Cory Marsh's *A Prime*
why, what, and ho͟w ͟ ͟ ͟ ͟s͟t͟u͟d͟y͟i͟n͟g ͟ ͟G͟o͟d͟'͟s ͟ ͟W͟o͟r͟d͟.͟ ͟M͟a͟r͟s͟h
persuasively argues that we need to be aware of what Scripture
teaches and proficient in interpreting and applying it. Highly
recommended!

Dr. Andreas J. Köstenberger
Leading evangelical scholar, co-founder of Biblical Foundations,
and author of
Invitation to Biblical Interpretation

Cory Marsh's primer on biblical literacy is a sprightly, clear,
engaging, faithful introduction to biblical hermeneutics. It pays
attention to the standard issues: the importance of genre and of
authorial intent, the place of the biblical languages, and the
essential role played by context. The work is solidly evangelical
without being caught up in debates over particular
denominational viewpoints. Footnotes show that Marsh has
been academically responsible, and his journey through the
interpretation of two commonly abused passages—Jeremiah
29:11 ("I know the plans I have for you") and Philippians 4:13
("I can do all things through Christ")—was especially well done.
Marsh also includes the *Chicago Statement on Biblical Inerrancy*
as an appendix, which I feel is a brilliant addition. Lay learners
need to know that previous generations of evangelicals have
thought carefully through matters of bibliology. This is a book
to work through with a new believer, or with someone just
getting into Bible study.

Dr. Mark Ward
Editor, *Bible Study Magazine*
and author of
Authorized: The Use and Misuse of the King James Bible

I am confident that we are once again living in an age of biblical illiteracy that we have not seen the likes of since the Dark Ages. Although the work of the Reformers brought the Church *ad fontes*, and in our current age we have the proliferation of Bibles in multiple translations and digital editions, we are once again meandering in the darkness without the light—both outside of the Church as well as within it. Dr. Marsh's book is a wonderful introduction to the need for biblical literacy. While walking the line of an accessible, yet well-researched primer, he has sounded the call for a return back to the Bible and given his readers many reasons why they should do so. I highly commend it to you.

Dr. Richard Bargas
Executive Director, IFCA International

Millions of people have been led astray by Bible-hijackers who distort the Word of God and prey on the biblically illiterate. Because of this, Cory Marsh has written a compelling resource that shows why it is critical for Christians to rightly understand the Bible, and how they can proficiently interpret its meaning. *A Primer on Biblical Literacy* encourages all Christians to handle Scripture with care and gives them the confidence that they can do so! I cannot recommend this resource more highly.

Pastor Ryan Day
Revolve Bible Church, San Juan Capistrano

A PRIMER ON

BIBLICAL LITERACY

DR. CORY M. MARSH

A Primer on Biblical Literacy
@2022 Cory M. Marsh
Published by Southern California Seminary Press
El Cajon, CA
ISBN: 978-0980644289

Edited by Joan Shim.
Layout by Jennifer Ewing.
Cover design by Jonathan Pasquariello.

DEDICATION

To the saints in Christ Jesus who are at Revolve Bible Church, along with the overseers and deacons.

To the students at Southern California Seminary who trust us to train them in the Scriptures, along with the faculty and staff who understand their "job" as a calling.

To the memory of my first teacher in the biblical languages, the late Dr. Thomas Rohm, who forever changed my view of the Bible with a single sentence: "There is nothing incidental in Scripture."

FOREWORD

Dr. Cory Marsh has provided the church with a resource that the Academy needed to provide. The Academy is where the Bible is studied with care. The Church is where believers meet for fellowship and growth as a body. In our culture today the missing link is often biblical literacy. And so, to begin with a primer that is persuasive and informative is a suitable help for fellow believers. Our family has seen that need. Two of our sons met for lunch. The older brother was suffering the pain of a troubled relationship. So, at lunch it was a running lament. His brother was a good listener. The younger brother is blessed with a supportive marriage, but he has himself suffered a lifelong health problem. After the meal was completed, he emailed his brother with Scriptures that had helped him in his need. He prayed that the Scriptures would help his brother. Sometime later, the older brother told me how helpful the Scripture was to him. And I thought how appropriate is biblical literacy. The younger brother was aware of the ministry of Scripture in his life and was proficient in understanding and sharing it with his brother who was hurting. Dr. Marsh's *A Primer on Biblical Literacy* can help others just like my sons who hurt themselves and need to help hurting brothers. I'm thankful for this resource bridging the gap.

Dr. Elliot E. Johnson
Senior Professor Emeritus of Bible Exposition,
Dallas Theological Seminary and author of
Expository Hermeneutics: An Introduction

PREFACE

This small book was birthed at the ground level of church ministry. It initially started as a series of blog posts I wrote for my local church—Revolve Bible Church (RBC) in San Juan Capistrano, California—where I serve on the extended leadership team. I also serve as a full-time professor at Southern California Seminary where I assign the Bible as the primary "textbook" in every course I teach.[1] Because the elders of my church know that I aim to bridge the worlds of church ministry and Christian scholarship, they asked me to produce an accessible narration on the importance of *biblical literacy*. This I was more than happy to do, since for some time now I have felt (and statistics bear out) that American evangelicals have become woefully ignorant of the very Scriptures they hold to be inspired and inerrant. If Christians really believe the Bible to be God's Word, then understanding the Bible should be their top priority.

Of course, this idea is not uniquely mine, as the Protestant faith itself was founded upon the necessity of

---

[1] I am reminded of John Sailhamer's outstanding academic vision of seminary being a "textual community," meaning every single course should be centered on, and an extension of, the text of Scripture. I'm happy to say this vision is shared by SCS. See Ched Spellman and Jason K. Lee, eds., *The Seminary as a Textual Community: Exploring John Sailhamer's Vision for Theological Education* (Dallas: Fontes, 2021).

studying and defending the Scriptures. On April 24, 1555, George Marsh became one of the earliest martyrs of the English Reformation under "Bloody Mary" Tudor in Chester, England. Marsh was sought out and burned alive by those loyal to the Roman Catholic queen for his unwavering stance on the Bible above all human authorities (the Reformation principle known as *sola Scriptura*—Scripture alone). While imprisoned in a dungeon awaiting his execution, Marsh wrote to several friends, encouraging them to remain steadfast in the Scriptures while also bemoaning the starvation of those who were kept from the nourishment of God's Word:

> As the true worshippers, serve ye God in spirit and verity, according to his sacred Scriptures, which I would wish and will you above all things continually and reverently (as both St. Paul and Christ command you) to search and read, with the wholesome monitions of the same; to teach, exhort, comfort, and edify one another, and your brethren and neighbours, now in the time of this our miserable captivity, and great famishment of souls, for want of the food of God's word.[2]

---

[2] George Marsh, "A Letter of George Marsh to Jenkin Crampton and Others," in John Foxe, *The Acts and Monuments of the Christian Church*, ed. by John Cumming (n.p., 1851, abridgement of the original English edition, 1563), The Ex-Classics Web Site, https://www.exclassics.com/foxe/foxe281.htm.

Marsh

As Marsh saw it, true Christians cling to the Scriptures "above all things," even when threatened with death. The "miserable" ones were those who were illiterate in the Word of God. As this Marsh shares the same conviction of that one (yes, he is a distant relative), I simply could not imagine a topic more important than biblical literacy. With that in mind, I set out to answer the question: *What is biblical literacy?* However, it turns out that tackling the subject is not as easy as it sounds. Hardly anyone directly addresses or defines the topic "biblical literacy" (a problem I discuss in Chapter Two). I quickly realized it is a concept largely *assumed* rather than explained. So, what I thought would be a simple blog post turned into a miniseries addressing *why* Christians should even be interested in becoming biblically literate, *what* biblical literacy is, and *how* Christians can achieve a level of biblical literacy with confidence. After completing this series for RBC, I was incredibly encouraged by the feedback I received from the saints, who explained to me how each blog was helpful to them in different ways. From that point, and with further encouragement from Dr. James Fazio and the team at SCS Press, I decided to expand that series into the brief book you are now reading. While I have revised and expanded the original blog posts with additional material and sources, making it a little more conducive perhaps for students in classroom settings (especially Chapter Three), I have intentionally kept this book accessible for novice and "rusty" Bible students of all levels. As such, this brief volume reflects both popular-level and academic influences.

In short, what I offer in the following pages is a primer or basic introduction framed by the question: *What is biblical literacy?* It is in no way comprehensive or the final word on the matter, but instead a handy tool that addresses the importance of biblical literacy for all believers. The DNA of the book is divided into three simple chapters: Chapter 1 answers the question of *why* Christians need to be biblically literate, illustrated by horrific examples of those who were not. Chapter 2 defines *what* biblical literacy actually is and what is required of the Christian to be genuinely literate in Scripture. Finally, Chapter 3 discusses the *how* of biblical literacy by explaining the importance of correct biblical hermeneutics and its application.

TABLE OF CONTENTS

FIGURES

INTRODUCTION

Our Legacy as People of The Book

A guiding principle throughout this book is that the Bible can (and should) be understood. To "reveal" something is to intend for it to be grasped, and the Bible is the written *revelation* of God. It has been *revealed* to us and we are to understand it. It stands to reason that if God revealed himself in the Bible, then He would want us to understand the Bible, since to know the Bible is to know the God of the Bible. While interpretive challenges inevitably confront every reader of Scripture, these are not barriers blocking a grasp of its clear teaching. Paul declared to the church at Corinth that God's character is not confusing but orderly (1 Cor 14:33). The Scriptures reflect God's character.

Indeed, there is a reason why Christians are known historically as "people of the Book."[1] The Bible functions as the Christian's sole authority for theology and life, and therefore "whatever the Bible teaches on some topic or

---

[1] See the excellent collection of essays in Jennifer Powell McNutt and David Lauber, eds., *The People's Book: The Reformation and the Bible* (Downers Grove: IVP, 2017).

another binds the Christian's conscience."[2] Such is the very essence of *sola Scriptura*—"Scripture alone." The Bible is our heritage. Our legacy is to read it, cherish it, and defend it—even with our lives.[3] But to do so with confidence, we must become biblically literate.

Before diving into the various contours of biblical literacy, I feel it's important at the outset to clarify what this book *does* and *does not* intend to do.

First, it does not aim to shame Christians into reading more of their Bibles. Personal reasons behind one's diet of biblical truth vary and, more times than not, "well-meaning Christians simply do not know where to begin."[4] Integrity demands that all Christians, even the most mature believer, acknowledge the Bible is pretty big, very old, and rather intimidating. If it really is God's Word "breathed out" (2 Tim 3:16), we should expect Scripture to be a little mysterious, even complicated at times. After all, the infinite God is its divine author, and this same God dwells in "unapproachable

---

[2] Steven B. Cowan and Terry L. Wilder eds., *In Defense of the Bible: A Comprehensive Apologetic for the Authority of Scripture* (Nashville: B&H Academic, 2013), 3.

[3] The classic Protestant text on those martyred for their Christian faith and conviction over Scripture is John Foxe's *Book of Martyrs*, originally published in England in 1563 as *Actes and Monuments of these Latter and Perillous Days, Touching Matters of the Church.*

[4] Ronnie Winterton, "A Practical Plan for Growing in Bible Literacy," Center for Faith and Culture, February 5, 2019, https://cfc.sebts .edu/faith-and-culture/practical-tips-for-growing-in-bible-literacy/.

light" (1 Tim 6:16). He is not a Rubik's Cube to solve, and neither are the Scriptures. The Bible is comprised of an entire library of ancient literature, some of which simply remains unsolved, and that might scare some people. So, it is understandable that when Christians are too overwhelmed or intimidated by the prospect of seriously reading Scripture, they refrain from even getting started.

However, it is equally true that laziness is often the culprit behind a Christian's lack of biblical literacy. Again, if we're honest, it's much easier to sit back and passively "be fed" by a solid preacher or entertained by a magnetic speaker who appears to know Scripture better than us. The excuse becomes: they've done the work, so we don't have to. Here, a reminder of the Bereans in Acts 17 is pertinent. They didn't allow even the apostle Paul's sermon to go by unvetted—and were described as "more noble" for doing so (v. 11). Therefore, challenges to one's familiarity with Scripture (or lack thereof) should be welcomed, not repelled.

Second, this book is not intended to be a technical work on hermeneutics. There are plenty of worthwhile treatments available on the technicalities of interpretive theory and methods, many of which are commended in the footnotes and in the Recommended Resources in the Appendices. While this small volume does indeed devote a chapter to hermeneutics, it is meant as an entry-level discussion on the subject and should be considered merely supplemental to one's assigned or preferred textbook on hermeneutics. This book is devoted to *biblical literacy*, which I view as a bigger subject than hermeneutics. If one were to imagine a Major

League Baseball game in progress, *hermeneutics* would be the diamond with its three bases and a pitcher's mound, while *biblical literacy* would be the packed stadium and property enveloping it all. Hermeneutics is certainly critical, but it is not an end to itself. Hermeneutics supports the bigger goal of helping the Christian gain awareness and proficiency in Scripture to become biblically literate.

Now, a word on what this book *does* aim to do. This small treatise on biblical literacy is a modest attempt at bridging the church and academia on a crucial subject without the erudition or condescension that often appears in such books. Christian authors must usually choose—with enforcement by their publisher—that their book targets *either* those in the church (and be expressed in terms suitable for a fourth grader) *or* scholars in the field (who then are the only ones able to access or understand its contents). This book, while certainly not expressed in scholarly jargon or overwhelmed with endless footnotes, is intended to be accessible for *any* Christian at *any* level while rejecting the customary pressure to "dumb it down." To borrow from Robert Plummer's aim in his fine textbook, "My goal was to be accessible without being simplistic and scholarly without being pedantic."[5] While the pendulum of this book swings more clearly on the side of accessible, I did write it with an eye toward some important scholarship on the matters it

---

[5] Robert L. Plummer, *40 Questions About Interpreting the Bible* 2nd ed. (Grand Rapids: Kregel Academic, 2021), 13.

addresses. Those interested in these debates are encouraged to consult the academic voices referenced in footnotes throughout the volume, as well as in the Appendices.

I firmly believe Christian leaders should always seek to be clear and accessible while simultaneously being unafraid to equip those under their care with technical subjects. This of course assumes the Christian leader is himself equipped or at least familiar with the pressing subject. On that note, I do anticipate those who serve in leadership to be among my readers along with the Christians in the pews as well as first-year seminary students. In writing this volume, I have considered these parties equally, but with a sharper focus on those who are less familiar with bibliology and hermeneutics.

As I disclosed in the Preface, this book was originally conceived in the church where I serve, Revolve Bible Church in south Orange County. It began as a blog series that Pastor Ryan Day asked me to write due to a recent amendment to our church's vision statement: "faithfully committed to biblical literacy."[6] What became clear to all was that if our church was serious about glorifying God and making disciples of Jesus, we needed to pursue biblical literacy. Though everyone agreed to this amendment, it did raise the

---

[6] The full statement is available at: Revolve Bible Church, "Core Values and Distinctives," https://revolvebiblechurch.org/about/core-values-distinctives. If memory serves, it was Faraz Haghighi who first audibly expressed the clause, "faithfully committed to biblical literacy" in a small room with several of us who responded with a resounding: Yes!

question: What exactly is biblical literacy? I wrote much of what follows with this group in mind.

On the same token, I am a full-time seminary professor at Southern California Seminary (SCS), where I regularly engage in the cutting edge of Christian scholarship and train others to become familiar (and hopefully interested!) in that world as well. In addition to courses on the New Testament, I teach beginning- to advanced-level classes on biblical interpretation and hermeneutical theory. The mission statement of SCS reads that the school is to glorify God "by assisting local churches to equip believers of various cultures." Our school's primary charge is, therefore, to support the *local church*, as it is through the church and not the seminary that the manifold wisdom of God is revealed (Eph 3:10). Indeed, the institution itself falls under the oversight of Shadow Mountain Community Church, a prominent local church in east county San Diego pastored by Dr. David Jeremiah. So along with the saints in my church, much of the book's contents have my students in mind as well—many of whom are working pastors, chaplains, missionaries, and budding scholars.

All of this is to say that this book was produced with the dual conviction of being grounded in the local church while informed by Christian scholarship. Consequently, I envision it to be used by first-year Bible college and seminary students as a (very) supplementary textbook in their hermeneutics courses *and* to be used and recommended by pastors and small group leaders in churches for their flocks to become more proficient in God's holy Word.

CHAPTER 1

WHY THE NEED FOR BIBLICAL LITERACY?

Ignoring the Past Repeats its Mistakes

Church historians can largely pinpoint eras that parallel the theological controversy of that day.[1] The earliest centuries following the close of the New Testament involved debates defending the Christian faith against both Jewish and pagan antagonists. Then came the great councils of the third through fifth centuries that articulated theological doctrines concerning the Godhead. For the next several hundred years, sophisticated doctrines of man, sin, and redemption became systematized leading to the greatest spiritual revival in Western history—the Protestant Reformation—in the sixteenth century. The doctrine of the church would continue to develop into the seventeenth through nineteenth centuries, along with the doctrine of end times which would result in a revival of premillennial thought in the twentieth

---

[1] A classic example is James Orr, *The Progress of Dogma* (London: Hodder and Stoughton, 1901). A more recent treatment is John D. Hannah, *Our Legacy: The History of Christian Doctrine* (Colorado Springs: NavPress, 2001).

century—the idea that Jesus will physically return to earth to establish a literal thousand-year kingdom in Israel.

It is interesting that modern systematic theology books order their contents in a way that largely mirrors how Christian doctrine progressed through history. Through it all, however, there is no exact historical period that gets classified with terms that evoke an overall doctrine of Scripture.[2] The canonization of Scripture (i.e., the gathering of authoritative books and letters that would result in our singular "Bible") took place during the first four hundred years of the Christian faith, and those same writings were appealed to as Christian theology developed throughout the ages. Yet there was never a century or two that was largely centered on knowing, studying, and formulating a doctrine of Scripture. Rather, one's comprehension of the Bible was largely assumed and used to formulate other theological doctrines.

If ever there was a perennial matter in the church that slips by untreated it is this: *biblical literacy.* In churches today, a Christian's awareness of and proficiency in Scripture (two elements explored later) are either assumed, designated for seminaries to address, or ignored altogether. Yet if every single Christian doctrine, belief, and hope finds its origin in

---

[2] Hannah does list "The Doctrine of Scripture, or Authority" as encompassing AD 150–400 but focuses this era on the development of the apostles' doctrine and the place of tradition vis-à-vis authority for early apologetics, not a period of Christians becoming literate in the Scriptures. See Hannah, *Our Legacy*, 29; 35–46.

the Bible, there can be no matter of greater import than for Christians to be biblically literate.

The Ancient Battle for the Bible

It is almost cliché in certain circles to claim the Bible is under attack. The truth is, the Bible has *always* been under attack. And, ironically, the most dangerous assaults on Scripture have historically come from those who are most familiar with it.[3] Consider the blitzkrieg Satan attempted on Jesus in Matthew 4:1–11. This incident marks the first exchange in the Bible between the Son of God and the devil. It also provides crucial lessons on the importance of correctly apprehending Scripture.

Jesus fasted for forty days and nights in isolation, and His human nature was at its weakest point. It was only then that Satan stepped in and ambushed Jesus with a barrage of temptations designed to break Him. After his first enticement for Jesus to turn rocks into bread, Jesus responds by directly quoting Scripture (vv. 3–4). Satan then changes his tactic to assault Jesus with the very same weapon Jesus just used on him. As S. Lewis Johnson observed, "Satan has

---

[3] For a penetrating study detailing the historiographical biases of biblical critics over the last three hundred years leading up to today's most popular opponent of the orthodox faith, see Jeremiah Mutie, *The Quest for Early Church Historiography: From Ferdinand C. Baur to Bart D. Ehrman and Beyond* (Eugene: Wipf & Stock, forthcoming).

learned something from the first test, namely, the importance of Holy Scripture to the Lord Jesus. So, this time he supports his request by the use of Scripture. But, in so doing he makes several mistakes."[4]

In the only example in all of the Bible of Satan directly quoting Scripture, he twists Psalm 91:11–12 *out of context* for his second assault on Jesus. In that passage, the psalmist says, "For He will command His angels to guard you in all your ways. On their hands they will bear you up lest you strike one foot against a stone." The portrayal of God is that of a loving protector who rescues those who trust in Him, expressed in poetic language (see v. 4). But Satan violates its literary genre and authorial intent in a clever move to tempt Jesus into physically jumping off the tallest point of the Jerusalem Temple (Matt 4:5–6). He was even sure to use the same introductory formula that Jesus used when appealing to the Bible, "it is written," just to prove that he too can appeal to the same source (v. 6; cf. 4, 7, 10). However, Jesus's response was the identical approach He used in each of the adversary's attempts to derail Him. Jesus cited passages from the Old Testament (particularly Deuteronomy) *in context* and did so maintaining their authorial intent. Incredibly, throughout the exchange, God's Word was the sword used by two polar opposite beings with two polar opposite methods.

---

[4] S. Lewis Johnson Jr., "The Temptation of Christ," *Bibliotheca Sacra* 123, no. 492 (Oct 1966): 347.

Not only was this event a battle between Jesus and Satan, it was also a battle for the Bible. Their exchange highlights the sobering fact that Scripture is equally the greatest weapon for harm *or* the greatest weapon for good depending on how it's used. Satan's technique of attacking God's Word by twisting it out of context is ancient. It is a ruse as old as creation—and is directly responsible for the fall of creation. Soon after God had given Adam and Eve the first command—not to eat from just one tree—the Serpent (identified as Satan in Revelation 12:9) subtly introduced the disastrous phenomenon of doubting God's Word: "Did God *really say* that?" (Gen 3:1). From this point forward, a plain or literal understanding of the Word of God that respected authorial intent would never hold the exclusive reign in biblical interpretation. Twisting Scripture out of its context is the ultimate subterfuge of God's enemies. From the beginning, the most treacherous offenders have been those most familiar with God's Word.

Fast forward thousands of years to the current era. The same evil ploy continues. And the results are, as they've always been, disastrous.

The Heisting of Scripture

November 18, 1978: A mass suicide of over 900 members of the Peoples Temple in Guyana, South America, ordered by their leader, Jim Jones—a narcissistic "Christian Marxist" who was ordained by the Independent Assemblies of God.

Jones reveled in titles like "pastor" and "reverend" while claiming to be the audible voice of God and personal fulfillment of Old Testament prophecies, such as the return of the prophet Elijah. Discovered among the pile of bodies were 304 children who were forced by their own parents to drink the group's cyanide-laced Flavor Aid following Jones's explicit commands to die together by "revolutionary suicide."

April 19, 1993: The horrific end to the "siege of Waco" in Texas as almost eighty members of the cultic Branch Davidians burned to death when their compound was set ablaze. Among the rubble were twenty-five children and two pregnant women (all practically unidentifiable) forced to their deaths by the group's leader, David Koresh—a delusional, false-prophet offshoot of Seventh-day Adventism who claimed to be the Lamb of Revelation 5 who alone was worthy to open the scroll.

March 26, 1997: San Diego sheriffs discover thirty-nine bodies all dressed the same as they lay in bunks scattered inside a rented mansion in Rancho Santa Fe, California. Such was the result of the ordered mass suicide by "Heaven's Gate" leader, Marshall Applewhite—a space alien enthusiast and former Presbyterian who, along with his co-leader Bonnie Nettles, identified as one of the two witnesses of Revelation 11. Together they taught that they were incarnations of Jesus and the Father. Later, Marshall claimed he was tasked to lead his followers by spacecraft to the kingdom of heaven, which he called, "the evolutionary level above human." There, the group would receive their glorified bodies, coinciding with the arrival of the Hale-Bopp comet.

Of course, these examples of Bible-heisters are the extreme. And of course there are others of equal infamy—from the recent "psychic surgeon" in Brazil, João Teixeira de Faria (referred to as "John of God"), guilty of innumerable sex crimes and medical malpractice while claiming to be a biblical prophet, to notorious false teachers of the past like Joseph Smith (Mormonism) and Joseph Franklin Rutherford (Jehovah's Witnesses).[5] The list of unqualified Bible teachers with cult followings stretches all the way back to the early second century with the first (in)famous "Christian" heretic Marcion, who butchered the unity of Scripture to the extent of seeing two opposing gods, one of the Old Testament and one of the New Testament.

Countless others who are more subtle have dotted history. Their ends may not include mass suicides or sieges, but they are equally dangerous. Indeed, their danger is precisely because of their subtlety compared to the Jim Joneses of the world. This sort run rampant in our day. Indulgent faith healers, prosperity gospel peddlers, and supposed prophets and apostles are a constant nuisance, as they twist Scripture out of joint to desperate crowds whose Bibles continue to collect dust (or whose apps gets crowded

---

[5] A classic volume on the various quasi-Christian cults that is most helpful is Walter Martin, *The Kingdom of the Cults: The Definitive Work on the Subject* 6th ed. (Bloomington: Bethany House, 2019).

by myriads of social media vanity). These groups are not led by humble men or women levelheaded enough to follow Paul's lead of referring to himself as a "slave" *before* he was an "apostle" (Rom 1:1). At times, the apostle was even satisfied with identifying himself solely by his slavery to Christ (see Galatians 1:10). Instead, these fraudsters delight in claiming apostleship and prophetic offices for themselves and intimidate their members from any challenge nearing an accurate understanding of Scripture.

For both groups, the average Christian is lower than laity. Their followers are cards in a fixed poker game. Unsuspecting people are cheated out of their money and any real spirituality while funding a con artist who's holding hidden aces and claiming to be a prophet or apostle. Ignoring Peter's and John's assurances that all true believers are priests before God who have the Spirit as their ultimate teacher (1 Pet 2:9; 1 John 2:27), these imposters keep their empires in check by warning against touching "the Lord's anointed"— another definitional heist that leverages a biblical idea out of context over enamored victims.[6]

Common Denominators

Diverse as these extreme to more subtle groups may be, they are connected in an unmistakable way: *each leader exploits*

---

[6] For an ex-insider's look see, Costi W. Hinn, *God, Greed, and the (Prosperity) Gospel* (Grand Rapids: Zondervan, 2019).

the Bible to the glory of themself and to the hopeless end of their followers. Familiar biblical terms, such as "kingdom of heaven," "witness," "Armageddon," "prophecy," "faith," and even "Jesus" and "Father," are often pilfered by these cultists to launch their own self-aggrandized agendas. They virtually take a hacksaw to the Scriptures, ravaging passages out of context and using them to level people who are too intimidated (or mesmerized) to speak up.

By mixing Christian theology with their own philosophies, each one creates a hybrid of bizarre and destructive yet intoxicating ideas (see Colossians 2:8). Like Gary Oldman's character Carnegie in the film *The Book of Eli*, each of these powermongers manipulate Scripture to their own desires while leaving behind mountains of scandal, shame, and trauma as their legacy. They each love to intoxicate their crowds. And they each exploit the Bible as the drug to do it.

An additional common denominator unites these groups: *the wolves are never held accountable to the Scriptures by their sheep.* Far from the typical caricature of the unsuspecting teenage hippie picked up by the Manson family (another cult whose leader abused the Bible to gain a following), such groups include highly educated politicians, business owners, civic leaders, even theologians. Remarkably, David Koresh had a loyal disciple to the fiery end who earned a PhD in Comparative Religion from the University of Hawaii. Dr. Steve Schneider served as Koresh's spokesman during the 51-day siege at Waco and was referred to as

Koresh's "chief lieutenant."[7] According to Byron Sage, one of the FBI's negotiators, "Schneider was educated. He was articulate, but he didn't have the independence of thought or the ability to do anything without the blessing of David."[8] Ultimately, Schneider's terminal degree in religion proved useless—even deadly.

The same can be said of Heaven's Gate leader Marshall Applewhite, who was educated in theology at Union Presbyterian Seminary and Jim Jones at Indiana University as well as at Butler University, where he earned his degree in secondary education. They took their academic exposure to the Bible and chose to exploit that knowledge rather than truly learn the Bible.

Using Scripture as a launchpad, Applewhite employed what some scholars have termed "UFO hermeneutics" to lure his followers into suicide and imaginary space life. Unmet with protest, Applewhite filtered the Bible "through a fundamental set of assumptions" that taught that alien life had interacted with earthlings in the past and would again in the future.[9] Distorting the biblical doctrine of rapture to an

---

[7] An insightful, accessible essay on Schneider's relationship to Koresh is Adriana Freedman, "Steve Schneider Was David Koresh's Spokesman During the Waco Tragedy," *Men's Health*, April 29, 2020, https://www.menshealth.com/entertainment/a32317580/steve-schneider-waco-netflix/.

[8] Ibid.

[9] Benjamin E. Zeller, "Extraterrestrial Biblical Hermeneutics and the Making of Heaven's Gate," *Nova Religio* 14 no. 2 (Nov 2010): 34–60.

unrecognizable level, Applewhite highjacked prophecies in the New Testament to justify bizarre beliefs that rivaled Hollywood's weirdest sci-fi plots. According to one study, "The founders and members of Heaven's Gate utilized the Bible to explain their beliefs, attract members, defend their religious positions, and ultimately to rationalize leaving their earthly bodies behind."[10] For Applewhite, the Bible was a fishhook he could manipulate in order to catch new recruits. His tactic is a shared one.

Jim Jones, who was trained at a university and seminary historically attached to the Disciples of Christ, favored exploiting passages from the Gospel of John through an idealist lens to recast his temple community as a minority persecuted for its socialism. From his skewed exegesis of John 14:12, Jones discouraged any prayer to God, deriding the Father as an uninterested "skygod," and taught that "Jesus's words and actions pointed toward the principle of socialism that would enable its followers to do greater things than Jesus did in the New Testament."[11] Once again, the Bible became a weapon in the wrong hands.

There is little doubt that each of these cultists' unbridled interaction with biblical themes significantly impacted their people's understanding of Scripture. Their tactics also barred their people from any semblance of a correct understanding

---

[10] Zeller, 35.

[11] Kristian D. Klippenstein, "Jones on Jesus: Who Is the Messiah?" *International Journal of Cultic Studies* 6 (Jan 2015): 41.

of *themselves* in light of Scripture. Like Satan, these speakers used the Bible to attack their audiences. But unlike Jesus's response to Satan, their audiences never held them accountable to the Bible. Instead of their flocks emulating the noble Bereans who carefully examined everything the apostle Paul taught in light of Scripture (Acts 17:11), these impressionable sheep swallow everything their wolves give them—even to death. Clearly, the results of heisting Scripture are devastating.

Doctrine of the Bible

Another common denominator unites each of the examples above but deserves its own section: *the need for a correct doctrine of the Bible.* In systematic terms, such a doctrine falls under the umbrella of *bibliology*, a mammoth of a topic that subsumes seemingly endless subtopics. This is not the place to exhaust such a subject; I've listed multiple excellent resources in this book's Appendices for those wanting to explore the worthwhile (and fascinating) contours of bibliology. Here, however, I feel it is important to point out the obvious fact that without an accurate doctrine, or belief, about the Bible, biblical literacy is in no way achievable. The false teachers above along with their crowds each testify to this as they all lacked a solid understanding of the very nature of Scripture.

In his final book, Francis Schaeffer cautioned Christians about abandoning a high, authoritative view of Scripture. For

Schaeffer, one's view of the Bible marks the watershed between Christian and non-Christian thought. Decrying what he foresaw as a "great evangelical disaster," he compelled believers never to abandon submission to Scripture's inspiration, inerrancy, and authority. "Holding to a strong view of Scripture or not holding to it is the watershed of the evangelical world," contended Schaeffer, "The first direction in which we must face is to say most lovingly but clearly: evangelicalism is not consistently evangelical *unless there is a line drawn* between those who take a full view of Scripture and those who do not."[12]

There are multiple implications stemming from believing (or not believing) that the Bible is inspired, inerrant, infallible, sufficient, and authoritative. Does the Bible *contain* or *become* the word of God, or is it the *actual* word of God? Have errors crept in that have corrupted its pure form? Were there errors in the original writings (called "autographs")? Does the Bible teach us all we need to know about life and salvation? Is it trustworthy? What place does Scripture have over my everyday life? These are all questions that are addressed in customary works centered on the doctrine of the Bible. While more will be said on this later, suffice to say here that the Bible declares itself to be the perfect word of God (Ps 119). It is "breathed out" (or inspired) by God and, therefore, entirely accurate and

---

[12] Francis A. Schaeffer, *The Great Evangelical Disaster* (Westchester: Crossway, 1984), 51.

trustworthy in its testimony (2 Tim 3:16). When Christians read in the New Testament that there is only one God and that Jesus is the only mediator between God and man (1 Tim 2:5), they will not allow any other person to compete for their loyalty as in the examples earlier. No one will come between them and God *because Scripture says* that only Jesus, the God-man, fills that role.

The most fundamental belief about the Bible is that it is God's written revelation. It is the result of Him actually *revealing* himself to humans. As Robert Plummer expressed, "The Bible itself is evidence of one of its main claims—that is, that God who made the heavens, the earth, and sea and everything in them is a communicator who delights to reveal himself to wayward humans."[13] Such a belief about the nature of Scripture is what connects the Christian to every other belief about God, creation, salvation, truth, and so on. In other words, the Bible being the revealed and thus authoritative Word of God is what grounds every other Christian doctrine.[14]

Though creeds and confessions are fallible (unlike Scripture), they can help us in the way we think about Scripture. One relatively modern confession that I

---

[13] Plummer, *40 Questions,* 20.

[14] David S. Dockery, *Christian Scripture: An Evangelical Perspective on Inspiration, Authority, and Interpretation* (Eugene, OR: Wipf & Stock, 1995), 1–14, rightly calls attention to what he labeled "the crises of biblical authority" in contemporary Christianity.

enthusiastically commend is the Chicago Statement on Biblical Inerrancy. Produced in the late 1970s by an incredibly diverse group of notable scholars and pastors, this document still serves as the primary statement for a conservative position on the nature of Scripture. Though not every Christian agrees with each of its nineteen articles, the statement does represent a sophisticated articulation of what evangelicals in the main believe about the Bible. Because of its helpful expressions and enduring impact on American evangelicalism, I have included it as an Appendix, along with other resources.

Dangerous Lessons

The Bible-hijackers above underscore a clear lesson: it is critical for Christians to understand the Bible. Biblical literacy can even become a matter of life and death. What would've changed if just one person who correctly understood Scripture's teaching on apostleship and prophecy had confronted David Koresh, who clearly did not? (See Acts 1:21–22 and 1 Cor 13:1–3; 14:29–33). What would've been the outcome if more parents in the Jonestown Massacre understood Scripture's explicit rejection of offering children to false gods and causes? (Lev 20:2–5; Jer 32:35). Imagine if a single member of Heaven's Gate actually took the time to look up references to "heaven" in the Bible and contrasted what it says about the throne room of God with the science fiction readings that Applewhite used to lure followers into his imaginary flying saucer? The examples may be extreme, but they are endless, and so are the more subtle cases confronting the average believer.

Space does not permit me to call out the errors of popular word-of-faith prosperity teachers who equally exploit the Bible and are given free rein to do so by their crowds. Names like Joel Osteen, Benny Hinn, Paula White, Bill Johnson, Kenneth Copeland, Todd White, and so on have become commonplace in such discussions. Those related to the recent New Apostolic Reformation and its Third/Fourth Wave charismania have been documented in accessible volumes.[15] These movements that promise healings and physical blessings in exchange for something certainly deserve to be called to task. However, a more urgent danger exists in the average pew every Sunday: *sincere Christians simply do not study the Bible for themselves.* They tend to be satisfied only with whatever their favorite preacher, Christian author, or podcast says about the Bible rather than examining it personally. Reminiscent of the Corinthians who organized factions around Apollos, Peter, and Paul—all of whom held to a high view of Scripture—they feel proud in saying: "I follow John MacArthur," "I follow David Jeremiah," "I follow Greg Laurie." The more erudite may take comfort in declaring: "I follow John Calvin," "I

---

[15] One solid example is, Costi W. Hinn and Anthony G. Wood, *Defining Deception: Freeing the Church from the Mystical-Miracle Movement* (El Cajon: SCS Press, 2018). A second edition with fresh content and accompanying study guide is forthcoming.

follow Charles Spurgeon," "I follow Wayne Grudem." In any event, they each follow their heroes without ever confirming if their heroes' instruction actually lines up with Scripture (thankfully, for the most part in these cases, they do!).

Another danger for the average Christian is to become dependent on mere spoonfuls of Scripture, like a daily devotional verse that's isolated from its context. Contrary to their subtle message, God did not drop the entire Bible out of heaven one verse at a time—and it's a good thing too. Early in my Christian walk, the verse to "claim" one day was: "And he said to him, 'All these I will give you, if you will fall down and worship me'" (Matt 4:9). The manufacturers of the devotional clearly never bothered to look up the passage. Had they done so, they would've discovered this verse is in fact the words of Satan as he was tempting Jesus to worship him! Laziness becomes a familiar culprit, keeping the average Christian from reading, learning, and savoring the entire passages in which individual verses are sandwiched.

In any case, the need for Christians to read, study, and reflect on the "whole counsel of God" has become tragically apparent in American evangelicalism, where polished one-liner tweets jockeying the Bible saturate a lucrative industry. Christians are called to make disciples of Jesus, not disciples dependent on themselves. Likewise, pastors and teachers are called to make disciples of Jesus, not disciples dependent on them. [16]

An Eerie Reminder

Facing the hundreds of bloated dead bodies at People's Temple in Guyana remained an empty wooden chair. The chair was once the throne of Jim Jones, where he would sit and declare lies and false prophecies to his disciples while holding a mic in one hand and, at times, a Bible in the other. Above that throne was a sign fastened to a wooden post that hung eerily over the pile of decaying flesh. The words that were neatly written on that sign in all caps thundered through the silence and stench:

THOSE WHO DO NOT
REMEMBER THE PAST
ARE CONDEMNED
TO REPEAT IT.

What an ironic and chilling reminder of the destruction that can result from misusing Scripture to one's own end.[17] While this is an extreme case, what's more relevant here is

---

[16] See Christopher Cone, *Integrating Exegesis and Exposition: Biblical Communication for Transformative Learning* (Ft. Worth: Exegetica, 2015), 37–40.

[17] The statement posted on the sign is an aphorism attributed to Spanish philosopher, George Santayana (1863–1952).

this: not one of the 909 people lying and rotting in homage to their leader had a Bible with them. Jones severely discouraged his members from packing Bibles to bring to the commune, and he possessed the only one among them of which he was aware. For everyone else, they were told to use the pages of Scripture as "toilet paper."[18]

This being the case, a remarkable discovery was made after the mass suicide. Of the seven thousand articles authorities inventoried, fifteen of them were in fact Bibles.[19] It is believed this tiny representation of God's truth was smuggled in by individual members, as no Bibles were cataloged in their community library. Tragically, these Bibles lay hidden and molded, mirroring their owners' use of them.

When I came upon this little-known detail of the People's Temple tragedy in preparation for this book, I became haunted by this question: *What would've changed if these fifteen Bible smugglers knew enough of their own Bibles to flock to one another and challenge every bit of Jones's demonically abusive teaching?* Even though they were warned not to bring Bibles, they must have held on to some truth of Scripture to risk smuggling it into that hell. Had they followed the counsel of Hebrews 10:24–25, which instructs Christians to meet together and encourage one another, they

---

[18] "Did People Have Bibles in Jonestown?" Alternative Considerations of Jonestown & People's Temple, San Diego State University, Special Collections of Library and Information Access, February 9, 2018, https://jonestown.sdsu.edu/?page_id=78266.

[19] Ibid.

would have been more attentive to Jones's willful ripping of passages out of the same book and twisting of them to his own glory. Maybe they would have continued reading together the next several verses that grippingly describe men like their "Reverend" who know the truth but deliberately reject it. Such people are not in fact covered by Jesus's sacrifice (vv. 26–31). They would've then known that the destiny of this wolf in their midst was a "fearful expectation of judgment, and a fury of fire" that will consume any adversary of Christ (v. 27). Had they actually believed these scriptural truths, they would not have killed their own children and themselves for the sake of a madman. Scripture declares itself to be effective for reproving and correcting those who oppose or misuse it and equipping the one who sincerely applies it (2 Tim 3:16)—something this group dreadfully failed to do.

Hence, we see the crucial importance of *biblical literacy* and its place in the local church. This will be discussed further in Chapter 2, as I will offer an explicit definition of biblical literacy and explain its purpose and goals—along with what is required on the Christian's part to be biblically literate.

CHAPTER 2

WHAT IS BIBLICAL LITERACY?

Achievable Awareness and Proficiency

Chapter 1 gave some dreadful examples illustrating why
biblical literacy is a fundamental need in the church. An
important idea emerged that to ignore the past is to repeat its
mistakes. History has proven that when charismatic personas
heist the Bible with promises of utopia on earth, the end is
disappointment, even destruction. History has also
demonstrated that it takes just one gullible follower to allow
attractive heresies into the fold before that aberrant teaching
takes over the fold. Highlighting the danger, Paul, in his very
first pastoral charge to his protégé Timothy, wrote with
fervency to "stop men from teaching strange doctrine" (1
Tim 1:3). The compound Paul used is ἑτεροδιδασκαλέω
(*heterodidaskaleō*, "heterodox teaching"), or in other words,
different or false doctrine.[1] Contrary to Scripture, strange,

---

[1] Cf. Walter Bauer, et al., *A Greek-English Lexicon of the New
Testament and Other Early Christian Literature*, 3rd ed. (Chicago:
University of Chicago Press, 2000), 399; Franco Montanari, *The Brill
Dictionary of Ancient Greek*, ed. by Madeleine Goh and Chad Schroeder

even bizarre, teaching was beginning to captivate this local church in Ephesus. The apostle knew it was only a matter of time before the wolves devoured the sheep with it. Something had to be done. Something can be done.

A church that is biblically literate is a church that safeguards God's Word from being distorted. Christians who have a solid grasp of biblical theology will recognize something is off if a polished speaker should step into a pulpit or lead a small group with doctrine that seems contrary to that of "the faith" (cf. Jude 3). But what does it mean to be biblically literate? This chapter will answer that question by explaining the "what" of biblical literacy along with what is required of the Christian to be genuinely literate in Scripture. But first, a few problems must be addressed.

The Problem of Definition

It is precisely at this first stage where a problem emerges. There is no agreed upon definition for "biblical literacy." While there exists some popular works that explore biblical literacy in helpful ways,[2] as well as unhelpful critical-

---

(Leiden: Brill, 2015), 833. Hereafter, these resources will be refenced as BDAG and MGS, respectively.

[2] Some recent, helpful examples are Dave Jenkins, *The Word Explored: The Problem of Biblical Illiteracy & What to Do about It* (Peterborough: House to House, 2021); and, Celina Durgin, "Are You Bible-Literate? How about Bible-Fluent? These Terms, Explained," The

scholarly discussions that use the term,[3] there is no general consensus or recognized standard definition for the phrase. Rather, biblical literacy is something mostly assumed. The problem is exemplified by Cecil Murphey's reference work actually called *The Dictionary of Biblical Literacy* which defines just about every term and concept related to Scripture except biblical literacy.[4] Moreover, when the concept of biblical literacy is addressed, it is usually presented in negative terms resonant with problems of biblical *illiteracy*. This can be seen in the various sources referenced in this chapter.

There is an unfortunate balance. The lack of published works that positively address, define, and promote biblical literacy seems proportionate with the lack of biblical literacy itself in America. Textbooks published on hermeneutics are in no short supply, and many of them appear in the final portion of this book (hermeneutics is the central focus of Chapter 3). The same cannot be said of textbooks published

---

Biblical Mind, February 18, 2021, https://hebraicthought.org/bible-literacy-fluency-explainer/.

[3] A notable example is the late Robert W. Funk who founded Westar Institute and the Jesus Seminar to promote "biblical literacy," both of which ultimately promote skepticism in the historical veracity of the Bible.

[4] Cecil B. Murphey, *The Dictionary of Biblical Literacy: Essential Information on the Bible, Biblical Culture, and the Church: Its History, Ideas, and Major Personalities* (Nashville: Thomas Nelson, 1989). See also, J. Stephen Lang, *Everyday Biblical Literacy: The Essential Guide to Biblical Allusions in Art, Literature and Life* (New York: Writer's Digest, 2007).

on biblical literacy.[5] I suspect the reason may be that hermeneutics is thought to overlap with biblical literacy to the extent that authors assume they are addressing both when they are really discussing only one. As I mentioned in the Introduction, I draw a distinction between the two and consider biblical literacy to be the larger subject. I view hermeneutics as an (essential) avenue to biblical literacy. In other words, the goal of hermeneutics is, as I see it, to give Christians the necessary interpretive principles and skills to achieve the *greater* goal of becoming biblically literate. The lack of such a distinction no doubt results in the lack of a shared definition for biblical literacy. However, definition is not the only problem. Another one hits closer to home.

The Problem of Familiarity

Recent polls indicate that while over 80 percent of American Christians claim to believe the Bible is the inspired Word of

---

[5] Some may point to Cullen Schippe and Chuck Stetson, eds., *The Bible and Its Influence* (New York: BLP, 2005) published through the Bible Literacy Project (www.bibleliteracy.org). But this work, produced by an ambitiously ecumenical group, does not address biblical literacy *per se* and is more focused on promoting an academic study of the Bible in public schools. A better alternative for elementary to high school Bible related textbooks produced from a conservative biblical worldview is BJU Press (www.bjupress.com), though they too lack specific works dedicated to "biblical literacy."

God, half can't name even one of the four Gospels.[6] Foreseeing this trend, Howard Hendricks offered six reasons why people don't study their Bibles.[7] These can be summed up as: (1) irrelevance—they don't think "it works"; (2) technique—they don't know how; (3) insecurity—they think one must be a pastor or professionally trained; (4) busyness—they simply don't have the time; (5) critical—they don't believe the Bible is reliable; (6) uninterested—they view the Bible as boring. It is telling that none of these six reasons suggests a lack of access to Scripture. Everyone in twenty-first century America can obtain a Bible in some format.

The problem is not that we don't have enough Bibles. The problem is we've become too familiar with the Bibles we have. Ninety-one million Bibles are printed globally each year, and America boasts an embarrassing number of translations.[8] Ironically, a case can be made that the lack of biblical literacy is a result of the overabundance of Bibles and related products in America. Instead of promoting

---

[6] For more penetrating statistics, see Ed Stetzer, "The Epidemic of Biblical Illiteracy in Our Churches," *Christianity Today*, March 13, 2017, https://www.christianitytoday.com/pastors/2017/bible-engagement /epidemic-of-bible-illiteracy-in-our-churches.html.

[7] Howard G. Hendricks and William D. Hendricks, *Living by the Book: The Art and Science of Reading the Bible* (Chicago: Moody, 2007), 14–18.

[8] See Todd M. Johnson and Gina A. Zurlo, eds. *World Christian Database* (Leiden/Boston: Brill), accessed November 12, 2021, www.worldchristiandatabase.org.

communion with the living God through His living Word, we've turned the Bible into an industry of merchandise. There is no longer reverence or love for Scripture's metanarrative of God's glory progressing throughout its sixty-six books. It has become a charm to keep in the house for good luck and prosperity; it's there "just in case." We all know there's a Bible. They're everywhere. But that's about it. The adage rings true: familiarity breeds contempt.

If 81 percent of American Christians believe that "God helps those who help themselves," is a Bible verse, and 12 percent believe that Joan of Arc was Noah's wife, clearly something is wrong.[9] The stats only get worse among average American high school students (both Christian and non-Christian), whose overall knowledge of the Bible is, frankly, pathetic.[10] It doesn't fare much better for college students. With funding granted by the John Templeton Foundation, a 2005 study commissioned by the Bible Literacy Project surveyed thirty-four English professors at top-ranked American colleges and universities. A major finding was that the lack of biblical literacy among students resulted in not

---

[9] See R. Albert Mohler, Jr., "The Scandal of Biblical Illiteracy: It's Our Problem," Albert Mohler, January 20, 2016, https://albertmohler.com /2016/01/20/the-scandal-of-biblical-illiteracy-its-our-problem-4.

[10] See the examples provided by Bible Literacy Project, "Bible Literacy Report: What Do American Teens Need to Know and What Do They Know?" (New York: Bible Literacy Project, 2005), https://irp-cdn.multiscreensite.com/09ffa3b8/files/uploaded/BLRExecutive Summary.pdf.

just a lack of overall knowledge of the Bible but a lack of overall knowledge of Western culture. To exclude the Bible from student learning is to withhold a critical understanding of "the English language, English literature, history, art, music, or culture."[11] At virtually each stage of Indo-European history, which includes the US, the Bible is there, informing the culture.

There are over twelve hundred references to the Geneva Bible within Shakespeare's works alone that in turn use English words William Tyndale coined in his sixteenth-century translation of Scripture. We can thank Tyndale for now-common phrases like "my brother's keeper," "good Samaritan," "the spirit is willing, but the flesh is weak," "salt of the earth," "scapegoat, "atonement," and many more. It's not surprising that, almost without exception, professors from Brown, MIT, Harvard, Princeton, and other prestigious institutions viewed knowledge of the Bible as critical for a good education.[12] As one Northwestern professor put it, the [Bible] "is the most influential text in all of Western culture."[13]

---

[11] Bible Literacy Project, https://www.bibleliteracy.org/.

[12] Bible Literacy Project, "Bible Literacy Report II: What University Professors Say Incoming Students Need to Know" (New York: Bible Literacy Project, 2006), https://irp-cdn.multiscreensite.com/09ffa3b8/files /uploaded/BLR2ExecutiveSummary.pdf.

[13] Ibid.

How would an American understand the stunning appeal made to "their Creator" to justify human equality in the Declaration of Independence without knowing its source? What reverence can an art major have for Michelangelo's exquisite sculpture of David or breathtaking frescoes of biblical scenes on the ceiling of the Sistine Chapel without understanding where they originated—and why he picked the ones he did? Can one truly understand Leonardo da Vinci's world-famous Last Supper portrait without knowing the scene in John's Gospel that inspired it?

In a country that from its origin until now has been relentlessly influenced by Scripture and the church, such biblical illiteracy is not the government's problem—it's our problem. It's an evangelical problem. We've allowed celebrity pastors to run wild with building their own platforms. Church "outreach" now rivals the most secular practices in marketing and branding. Taking the front seat are conferences and podcasts. Taking the back seat—if not the trunk—is the Bible. Tragically, Scripture is no longer valued as the premier source for learning. It has oddly become trivialized by the very people who historically formed around the highest view of God's Word. In a culture whose heroes offer cheap thanks to God and passionately declare, "I'm going to Disneyland!" in the same breath, it's hard not to notice the Holy Bible being trivialized—and God along with it.

It is certainly our problem, but it is fixable. Christians need to get vintage. Churches need to ensure their top priority is old fashioned—to train their people in Bible. Such is the impetus for growing in love for Christ, because biblical literacy results in more love for the God of the Bible. But to achieve biblical literacy, we must nail down what it even means to be biblically literate and how we get there.

Biblical Literacy Is *Awareness* and *Proficiency*

Being biblically literate does not mean that the Christian has gained mastery over all of Scripture's contents. The goal is more modest than that. In my experience, biblical literacy centers on two key ideas: *awareness* and *proficiency*. Awareness and proficiency are always attainable; technical expertise is not. Therefore, biblical literacy is achievable for every Christian.

Biblically literate Christians progressively develop in their *awareness* of the God of the universe by reading through the Scriptures while gaining *proficiency* in their understanding of Scripture's meaning. In other words, biblical literacy is achieved when the Christian is able to recognize the various historical contexts and literary genres in Scripture that God used to reveal Himself and, from there, can discern the Scripture's meaning expressed through those contexts. Increased *awareness* and *proficiency* is the goal of biblical literacy as well as the guide rails for responsible application.

The biblically aware Christian no longer views the Bible as a single book but as an *entire library* of distinct literary forms spread across thousands of years of world history.

Particularly, awareness develops as recognition of literary genres increases. Elliot Johnson describes this recognition as "active" reading. Unlike passive, mindless reading for pleasure, active reading of Scripture "is a process of thinking, questioning, formulating and reconsidering that leads to a dawning awareness of the sense as a whole text that fits all the parts of it."[14] There is no biblical text that is an island to itself. Every portion, regardless of its distinct genre, fits together with the greater whole. On the same token, each portion's distinct genre will be recognized and respected for what it is. History will be recognized as history, poetry recognized as poetry, epistle recognized as epistle, and so on.[15]

This means that one who is biblically literate understands there is an obvious difference in form and expression between Scripture's historical narratives, like Genesis or Acts, and poetic books, like Psalms or Song of Solomon. With an increased awareness of the Bible's array of literary genres, no longer will the Gospels be read in the same manner as Paul's letters or even Revelation. Their distinct forms of biography, epistle, and prophecy will be respected as well as their historical contexts—such as Jesus's prime audience being Israel and Paul's audience the church. Distinctions (often called "discontinuity") between the Old

---

[14] Elliot E. Johnson, *Expository Hermeneutics: An Introduction* (Grand Rapids: Zondervan, 1990), 81.

[15] See *The Chicago Statement on Biblical Inerrancy*, III.C, reprinted in the Appendices.

Testament and New Testament become cherished, not feared or fought, as does Scripture's continuity—shown brilliantly in God's glory and grace tying up all of world history with Christ as the centerpiece.

With proficiency comes knowledge of the Bible's key themes, characters, stories, and order of events. John's emphasis on glory, Paul's emphasis on faith, and Peter's emphasis on hope become pivots in the New Testament, as do the themes of exodus, law, and covenant in the Old Testament. The biblically proficient Christian comes to view the Bible's meticulous details as "scaffolding" that supports an overarching framework.[16] Basic background information for individual books of Scripture—like its author, possible dates of composition, its purpose, and its original destination—helps reorient the twenty-first-century reader from any cultural blind spots to the ancient times of the Bible. Repeating this process for every book of the Bible secures its scaffolding, and a narrative arc becomes apparent: *God's glory expressed from creation through fall through redemption and finally through consummation.* As a result, the biblically proficient Christian understands that the Bible is far from disjointed or fragmented. What becomes clear is the Bible's

---

[16] I borrow this metaphor from George H. Guthrie, "The Study of Holy Scripture and the Work of Christian Higher Education," in *Christian Higher Education: Faith, Teaching, and Learning in the Evangelical Tradition,* ed. by David S. Dockery and Christopher W. Morgan (Wheaton: Crossway, 2018), 92–94.

plumbline of God's glory connecting Genesis to Revelation through Jesus Christ.

The Correct Posture for Biblical Literacy

If increasing in awareness of the Bible's literary genres and gaining proficiency in Scripture's teaching is the skill of biblical literacy, is there an underlying posture or attitude that allows such literacy to be achieved? Yes, there is—and it's crucial. Too often pride inflicts the astute Bible reader into thinking they know all there is to know about Scripture. Familiarity with beloved stories like Jonah and the great fish, David and Goliath, or Jesus and the raising of Lazarus can trick people into thinking they can't learn anything new. But, as Daniel Doriani contends, "To profit from Scripture, one must take the right posture."[17] In adopting the right posture to achieve biblical literacy, two extremes will be avoided.

The first is approaching the Bible with such skepticism that virtually everything in its pages is judged, critiqued, or must be "proven" to the reader's satisfaction. The other extreme is to approach the Bible with overconfidence, so convinced by their favorite preacher or theological system's use of a passage that they choose to ignore any other

---

[17] Daniel Doriani, "Interpreting the Bible: An Introduction," in *Understanding Scripture: An Overview of the Bible's Origin, Reliability, and Meaning*, ed. by Wayne Grudem, C. John Collins, and Thomas R. Schreiner (Wheaton: Crossway, 2012), 12.

possibility that may challenge their preconceived theology. Both instances trifle with the Bible and need to be avoided. Rather, a different attitude should envelop the committed Christian who sincerely desires to be biblically literate. The correct posture is one infused with a healthy dose of fear for the living God, who at times has appeared as a consuming fire and by His great mercy has breathed out His living word for us to know Him.

The Requirements of Biblical Literacy

Biblical literacy is important not only to safeguard Scripture from being hijacked by cultists and false teachers (as discussed in Chapter 1) but also for the believer to grow closer to God. A Christian's relationship with God is directly proportionate to their relationship with God's Word. Examples abound in Scripture that to love God is to "keep" His Word and that to "hear" His Word means to obey it. For the Christian to become biblically literate, therefore, certain essentials must first be in place—and they are all existential. Here, I will discuss five character-focused requirements for biblical literacy. They include being regenerate, prayerful, humble, obedient, and diligent.

First and foremost, true biblical literacy can only be achieved by someone who is a *genuine believer in Jesus Christ*. They are "Christian," not in name only but by their relationship to God through personal faith in Christ. In New Testament terms, this person is regenerated or "born again"

(John 3:3, 7; 1 Pet 1:3, 23). This means the Holy Spirit indwells them, leads them, unites them to other believers, and helps them in their understanding of all spiritual matters—including Scripture itself (John 16:12–14; 1 Cor 2:12–16; cf. 1 John 2:27). All other requirements are based on this one essential precondition.

Second, a *prayerful attitude* is necessary. As the psalmist prayed, "*Make me understand the way of your precepts*, and I will meditate on your wondrous works" (Ps 119:27, emphasis added). The Christian "looks up" to God for understanding before they "look down" to read His Word. Ultimately, it is God in Christ who opens minds to understand the Scriptures, making biblical literacy dependent on Him (cf. Luke 24:45).

Third, along with prayer, the Christian is to demonstrate *humility* (Jas 1:19). They should genuinely desire to learn from the Bible and be willing to readjust any preconceived beliefs that may conflict with Scripture's clear teaching.

Fourth, the Christian should *obey* Scripture's teaching where applicable. This is what James calls being a "doer" of the Word, echoing Jesus's penetrating remarks about those calling Him "Lord" while not actually "doing" what He says (Luke 6:46; Jas 1:22). Intellectual apprehension of the Bible can be attained by anyone, but only the Christian can submit to its divine authority.

Finally, *diligence* is the fifth necessary step in becoming biblically literate (2 Tim 2:15). The Christian is to make every effort before God to rightly handle His Word and gain His approval. Such diligence assumes integrity on the part of the believer and their reverence for the Scriptures. As Solomon declared thousands of years prior, a healthy fear of God is the very foundation of knowledge and wisdom (Prov 1:7; 9:10).

Taken together, the necessary requirements of biblical literacy are being born-again, maintaining a prayerful attitude, expressing genuine humility, demonstrating joyful obedience, and zealously striving for diligence. These are all very personal. There is also another vital element to consider which widens the focus past self to include others. It is often a missing factor in discussions on biblical literacy, but it is nevertheless crucial.

The Crucial X-Factor for Biblical Literacy

Biblical literacy leads not to fat heads or egos but to transformed lives that mature in their understanding of God and joyfully submit to the authority of Christ. This was the apostle Paul's main goal for the Colossian church (Col 1:28–29), and it should be the same for the evangelical church today. Moreover, Paul was clear that the goal or *telos* of Christian instruction codified in Scripture is *agapē*—"love" (1 Tim 1:5). This means the Christian will grow in their love for God, for mankind, and for overall learning as they become more literate in the Scriptures. So, there is reciprocity.

The more biblically literate the Christian becomes, the more spiritually mature they become since "spiritual maturity requires a high degree of biblical literacy."[18] Yet, there is an important link between the two that often goes unnoticed: *spiritual maturity and biblical literacy are connected by fellowship.* In other words, the premier avenue through which Christians develop both biblical literacy and spiritual maturity is in fellowship with other Christians. This is the crucial X-factor.

Micah Watson has rightly argued that the home and local church are the most important training grounds for biblical literacy, even over Christian schools. Generational discipleship centered on Scripture must begin in the family and church, which then produces the next generation of Christians.[19] The New Testament knows nothing of lone-ranger Christians. Never is one of Jesus's disciples portrayed as alone or isolated from one another.[20] They always learned and ministered together as a group under Jesus, or at least in triads or pairs. Likewise, Paul traveled with companions on each of his mission trips and as a new believer followed

---

[18] Cone, *Integrating Exegesis*, 42.

[19] Watson, "Faith, Ethics, and Culture" in *Christian Higher Education*, 474.

[20] A possible exception is the apostle John who was banished to Patmos where he received his revelation of Jesus Christ. Him being isolated from his church or other Christians was not John's choice, but due to persecution on "account of the word of God" (Rev 1:9). Though, nothing in the text precludes the possibility that John enjoyed fellowship with other Christians on the island.

Barnabas's lead. Aquila is never seen without Pricilla, and the two discipled Apollos. The list goes on. From this we can infer that Christians, especially newer believers, *develop their awareness and proficiency of Scripture in community with other Christians who are more seasoned in the Faith* (see Heb 10:24–25).

It is in contexts of personal discipleship and regular gathering among the saints that Christians most aptly learn the Bible's major connecting points and content. Assembling on the first day each week for worship and the faithful preaching of Scripture has been a premier avenue for learning the Bible ever since the birth of the church (Acts 2:42; cf. 20:7; 20:27). As Paul stated, it is "through *the church* that the manifold wisdom of God is made known" (Eph 3:10, emphasis added). For two millennia, discipleship and fellowship have proven to be essential resources for Christians to understand their own Christian faith. Believers encourage other believers in the Scriptures, motivated by their shared reverence for the Lord and love for His saints. Learning together, they begin to "own" their faith in God as Christianity moves from being conceptual or merely doctrinal to becoming radically personal. No longer are the Scriptures just the dusty old family Bible or the unreachable resource reserved for professional theologians. Like a pleasing aroma to the Lord, the level of biblical literacy rises in a church where members maintain consistent fellowship under the expositional preaching of the Word—and grow to love and defend the Scriptures with their very lives.

A Note on Languages

Before concluding, a question may arise at this point concerning the need to know the original languages of the Bible. *Is learning them necessary in order to achieve biblical literacy?* The simple answer is no. But the excessive surplus of English translations available in the US can mislead one to think that the Bible was originally written in English or, more commonly, that English is the best language through which to understand the Bible.[21]

The Bible was not originally written in English or any other modern language. It was almost entirely written in two ancient languages, divided by the two Testaments: the Old Testament in various forms of Hebrew and the New Testament in Koine Greek. While traces of both these languages live on in their modern forms, overall they are considered "dead" languages. That is, they are no longer spoken for daily communication.[22] In addition to ancient Hebrew and Greek, several brief parts of the Old Testament

---

[21] One fascinating study demonstrating the assistance that the Korean language provides *over* English in translating the biblical Hebrew אָנָּא (nāʾ) particle is, Bent Christensen, "A Linguistic Analysis of the Biblical Hebrew Particle nāʾ: A Test Case," *Vetus Testamentum* 59 (2009): 1–15. Christensen convincingly shows the need for general linguistics in Bible translation and how different languages provide help for translation by surfacing nuances in the biblical languages.

[22] This obviously excludes full-immersion language programs for ancient Hebrew, Aramaic, and Koine Greek.

were written in square script called Aramaic, a sister language to Hebrew used by various pagan tribes during the Old Testament period. Aramaic became an internationally shared language throughout the Ancient Near East, used for commerce and diplomacy (much like English today and Koine Greek in early centuries).[23] This particular "dead language" appears in only five places throughout the Old Testament (Ezra 4:8–6:18; 7:12–26; Jer 10:11; Dan 2:4–7:28, and two words in Gen 31:47). While Aramaic was still widely spoken in the days of Jesus, the oldest extant manuscripts of the New Testament are all in Koine Greek. So, the Bible was originally written in three languages: Hebrew, Aramaic, and Greek.

As someone who teaches the New Testament, I am very passionate about Christians learning the biblical languages. Part of my course load involves teaching New Testament Greek (Koine Greek) at all levels. When I was a student in seminary, I couldn't fathom graduating with a *Bible* degree without ever taking biblical Greek and Hebrew. It seemed obvious that if I really wanted to know the Bible, I should become familiar with the very languages in which it was written. I still think that. It is tragic how many seminaries continue to cut their language requirements from their degree programs. Learning Hebrew and Greek used to be the

---

[23] See Walter J. Martin, and K. A. Kitchen, "Language of the Old Testament, II. Aramaic," in *New Bible Dictionary,* 3rd ed., ed. by I. Howard Marshall, A. R. Millard, J. I. Packer, and D. J. Wiseman (Downers Grove, IL: IVP Academic, 2007), 668–669.

main reason an aspiring pastor would even enroll in seminary! That said, while I think nothing beats learning the biblical languages through an in-person intensive seminary course, there are an array of wonderful language tools available for *any* student of Scripture from which to learn Hebrew and Greek. I've listed several electronic sources in the Appendices that are reputable and trusted for learning the biblical languages, both paid subscriptions and free ones.[24]

Now let's get back to the question of whether learning these ancient languages is necessary in order to become biblically literate. As I said, the answer is no. It is entirely possible to grow in awareness and proficiency in Scripture (biblical literacy) without having ever studied the ancient languages in which the Bible was written. One of the many beauties that separates the Bible from other religious texts is that its message is not restricted to one language or location. It is typical Muslim belief, for example, that the Quran is only understandable in its original Arabic form. Any translation of this book is considered subpar and even impinging on how

---

[24] Here, I will only mention two others that are free and very helpful to begin immersing in the languages in small doses: Daily Dose of Greek (www.dailydoseofgreek.com) hosted by Robert Plummer, and Daily Dose of Hebrew (www.dailydoseofhebrew.com) hosted by Mark Futato, Adam Howell and Tom Blanchard. To this day, I subscribe to two-minute videos from both screencasts which have been an enjoyable help to me over the years, not only for keeping me on my toes in the languages, but also for seeing how I might relate those ideas in the classroom. I highly recommend both screencasts. There's no excuse—they're free!

(they believe) it was revealed to Muhammad. For them, the Quran is locked in Arabic. By contrast, the Holy Bible was never intended to be restricted to one language or one culture. It is God's Word, and its target audience is everybody everywhere! From as far back as the call of Abram (the father of all Semitic peoples) we read of promises that were intended for "all the families of the earth" (Gen 12:3). When Jesus commissioned His disciples, He told them, "Go make disciples of all nations" (Matt 28:19). Scripture was never intended to be shackled to a certain language or to a certain place in time.

The fact that God chose both Hebrew and Greek through which to inspire His Word is itself an amazing testimony to its divine origin. In one "book" exist two Testaments written over a fifteen-hundred-year time span by over forty authors spread over three separate continents. The languages they used just "happen" to be the most translatable languages in the world, and we're left with thousands upon thousands of ancient manuscripts with these languages for translators to compare and contrast. Hebrew in the East, Greek in the West—both global hemispheres together receiving God's holy words! From these languages, the Bible is more than capable of being translated accurately into any language on earth. As Mark Ward contends, "All Bible-loving-and-reading Christians need to learn to see the value in all good Bible translations."[25] As such, Christians should be confident in solid English translations while also avoiding tribalism over their preferred translations.

Our mainline English translations are trustworthy and accurately reflect the original writings of Scripture.[26] This should be no surprise if the Bible really is God's revealed will for the world. For, as the psalmist expressed: "Forever, O LORD, your word is firmly fixed in the heavens" (Ps 119:89). Indeed, no language on earth can restrict or thwart God's Word.

The Need for Consistent Biblical Literacy

The apostles were aware of how easily wolves dressed as sheep could arise in a local church. It happens through the infatuation of undiscerning Christians (cf. Acts 20:29; 2 Pet 2:1). Churches open the door to doctrine deviant to Scripture when they don't really allow Scripture to permeate all that they do—from the pulpit to the parking lot. Instead, they settle for an entertaining speaker. The music gets louder, the stage gets bigger, and the Bible gets smaller. Soon, general

---

[25] Mark Ward, *Authorized: The Use and Misuse of the King James Bible* (Bellingham: Lexham Press, 2018), 124.

[26] By "mainline" translations, I am referring to translations (not paraphrases or fringes) that are commonly accepted by evangelicals. These include, but are not limited to: KJV, NKJV, ESV, RSV, NASB, CSB, NIV, NET, NLT, LEB, and most recently, the LSB.

discernment becomes a relic of the past. "As shocking as it may sound," contends Richard Bargas, "some of those that are devoted to strong biblical doctrine on paper are not teaching and preaching the same from their pulpits and their Sunday schools. This spiritual anemia is yielding a weak church that is susceptible to many varieties of theological error."[27]

Bargas's diagnosis highlights the need for a consistent biblical literacy, not merely for the average Christian but for leaders in churches who claim to be Bible-centered and expository. The danger is real since a lack of biblical literacy among Christians results in a lack of biblical theology. For a Christian to be biblically *illiterate* is to open themself to the shifting tides of culture that tend to redefine biblical institutions such as marriage or even the family.

Such was the case recently with the 2015 US Supreme Court decision in Obergefell vs. Hodges, which appealed to reinterpreted constitutional rights for same-sex unions while overriding democratically enacted state definitions of traditional marriage.[28] The states of Michigan, Kentucky, Ohio, and Tennessee all defined marriage as a union between one man and one woman, and based it squarely on Scripture (Gen 2:24; Matt 19:4–5). But some appealed to these familiar verses—which have grounded a biblical theology of marriage

---

[27] Richard Bargas, "When Truth is Silent," *Voice* (Nov/Dec 2021): 7.

[28] See Obergefell, et al. vs. Hodges, Director, Ohio Department of Health, et al. No. 14-556 (June 26, 2015).

for thousands of years—and reinterpreted key words to mean something else. It worked. Dissenting the court's decision, Justice Scalia stated: "The law can recognize as marriage whatever sexual attachments and living arrangements it wishes, and can accord them favorable civil consequences."[29] His dissension was not based on an axe to grind against same-sex partners but the grave implications stemming from the US government's ability to effectively usurp a Higher Authority: "My Ruler, and the Ruler of 320 million Americans coast-to-coast, is a majority of the nine lawyers on the Supreme Court."[30] The court's decision became a watershed in the US by expanding the biblical definition of marriage and requiring all states to issue marriage licenses to same-sex couples. All of this began with a group of people who lacked any semblance of biblical literacy and, like Satan before them, cleverly misinterpreted biblical texts for their own agendas.

Once again, we are reminded of the need for all Christians—overseers, deacons, and saints—to sharpen one another in the Scriptures. Indeed, biblical literacy for the local church is an essential goal. Awareness and proficiency in approaching the text is achievable. All Christians can—and are expected to—achieve biblical literacy. But this raises the question: *How* does a Christian become biblically literate? The final chapter of this book will answer this by exploring

---

[29] Obergefell, et al. vs. Hodges.

[30] Ibid.

correct interpretative method, or *hermeneutics*. As chapter three argues, everything boils down to hermeneutics.

CHAPTER 3

HOW IS BIBLICAL LITERACY ACHIEVED?

Everything Boils Down to Hermeneutics

In the previous chapter, I defined "biblical literacy" by two key concepts: awareness and proficiency. Biblical literacy is achieved when the Christian can recognize Scripture's historical contexts and the literary genres that God used to reveal Himself (awareness) and, from there, discern the Scripture's meaning expressed through those contexts (proficiency). I also argued that because its goal is less ambitious than expertise or mastery, biblical literacy is achievable for—and expected of—every Christian. Moreover, I claimed that, ultimately, it is only a true believer in Jesus Christ who can become biblically literate, as submission to Scripture's divine authority is part and parcel of a true understanding the Bible (hence my use of "Christian" as the recurring subject in this book).

With a framework now in place that surveyed *why* biblical literacy is important and defined *what* biblical literacy is, this final chapter will explore the technicalities of *how* one becomes aware and proficient enough to achieve biblical literacy. As such, this chapter concerns interpretive method, also known as *hermeneutics*. By necessity, it will be the lengthiest chapter. One's method of interpreting Scripture is incredibly important as it will determine not only their theology but how they apply what they read. Indeed, *everything boils down to hermeneutics.*

Herman ... *Who?*

Hermeneutics is a funny sounding word. Spoken quickly, it sounds like someone's name, *Herman Neuticks*. But like much of the English language its origin is Greek, and its meaning is not as difficult as it may sound.

The word "hermeneutics" simply comes from the Greek verb *hermēneuō*, meaning "to interpret or translate."[1] Luke 24:27 reports, "And beginning with Moses and all the Prophets, Jesus interpreted [*hermēneuō*], to them in all the Scriptures the things concerning himself."[2] In John, Jesus told the blind man to "'Go wash in the pool of Siloam' (which translates [*hermēneuō*], 'Sent'). So, he went and washed and came back seeing" (9:7). Immediate context dictates which English word works best, "interpret" or "translate," since the former carries the idea of explanation in the same language while the latter swaps a word in one language for another in the target language (e.g., "Siloam" = "Sent."). In either case, it's the same Greek term and the general sense of the word is

---

[1] Cf. BDAG, 393; MGS, 525.

[2] Technically, the verb Luke uses, διερμηνεύω (*diermēneuō*), is simply an intensified form of *hermēneuō* meaning to "interpret through."

kept.[3] In English, we may use "mean" to get the same idea across. What someone *means* is how they should be interpreted or translated, i.e., *hermēneuō*.

The field of hermeneutics has a broad scope. In a general sense, it is the disciplinary study of the methods and history of interpretation of any corpus of literature (biblical or non-biblical). When used in discussions surrounding the literature of Scripture, the field is narrowed to "biblical hermeneutics." The discipline of biblical hermeneutics is, therefore, the study and practice of biblical interpretation. More specifically, *biblical hermeneutics is the science and art of interpreting the Bible.*[4] It is scientific because there are rules that help guide the process. It is artistic in that applying those rules depends on the interpreter's skill and, ultimately, the leading of the Holy Spirit. As it relates to biblical literacy, I am using the word "hermeneutics" to mean a method of interpreting the Bible that helps the Christian gain awareness and proficiency of Scripture in order to understand God's revealed will.

---

[3] The Greek word itself seems to have its origin in Greek mythology. "Hermes," the son of Zeus, was credited with discovering language and writing. The ancient Greeks considered Hermes to be the god of interpretation and eloquence as he transmitted messages from the gods to humans. This helps explain why the local populace called Paul "Hermes" in Acts 14:12.

[4] This definition is the consensus among conservative biblical scholars and most clearly articulated by Roy B. Zuck, *Basic Bible Interpretation* (Colorado Springs: David C. Cook, 1991), 19–22.

The Goal of Biblical Hermeneutics

In the mid twentieth century, Bernard Ramm stated the goal of biblical hermeneutics with clarity: "To ascertain what God has said in Sacred Scripture; to determine the meaning of the Word of God."[5] Again, God revealed His will in Scripture which implies that it can and should be understood. There is zero profit if God has spoken and Christians do not know what He said. Thankfully, God has spoken, and hermeneutics is the process of discerning or ascertaining what God has revealed or spoken in the Bible. What a passage of Scripture *means* is the question biblical hermeneutics seeks to answer.

A popular notion is that a Christian should read the Bible as they read any other type of literature. The idea is that the same rules of interpretation apply to all literature and the Bible is no exception. No one confuses tax documents with song lyrics, for example. An IRS 1040 is naturally understood according to its literary genre as is Johnny Cash's "Folsom Prison Blues" according to its genre. A person does not need to be told how they differ; it's obvious. If more people understood this principle of interpreting literature according to its genre and intention, Scripture would not suffer from so many misinterpretations by people who want it to mean whatever *they* want it to mean. There is, of course, truth to

---

[5] Bernard Ramm, *Protestant Biblical Interpretation*, rev. ed. (Grand Rapids: Baker, 1956), 2.

this "rule" and the intention is well-meaning. But it is not entirely accurate.

The Bible is not just any type of literature. It is the only literature in the world that is *theopneustos* or "God-breathed" (2 Tim 3:16). Moreover, it has dual authorship: divine and human. Peter stated that men wrote Scripture as they were "carried along" by the Holy Spirit (2 Pet 1:21). As such, the Bible is both the word of God and the word of man. As Jesus—the living Word—is both human and divine, the Bible—the written Word—is both human and divine. These dual natures are complementary, not contradictory.

Therefore, in regard to hermeneutics, the Bible is in a special class by itself. It cannot be read in the same way as any other type of literature.[6] It testifies to the glory of God throughout history, with Jesus Christ as the pinnacle of God's glory and world history (Heb 1:1–3). This makes the Bible infinitely greater than all the "sacred texts" of the world's great religions. While customary rules of interpretation are applied to Scripture in order to discern its meaning, this particular literature is "living and active" (Heb 4:12)—with eternal consequences weighing in the balance. Clearly, how a

---

[6] Contra R. Alan Culpepper, *Anatomy of the Fourth Gospel: A Study in Literary Design* (Philadelphia: Fortress, 1983/87), 10, who contended "Scripture must be studied with the same methods that are applied to the study of 'secular' literature." To his credit, Culpepper was defending a synchronic approach to the text against diachronic advocates who thought reconstructing the compositional process of John's Gospel was more important than the experience of reading the text.

Christian interprets the Bible is radically more important than how they interpret anything else.

The Meaning of "Meaning"

If the goal of biblical hermeneutics is to discover or ascertain the *meaning* of Scripture, then it begs the question: *What is "meaning"?* Some argue that meaning is inherent in the text *as text*. That is, the text is an autonomous entity to itself, and meaning is sourced in the linguistic symbols and syntax (or words and sentences) apart from the person who wrote them.[7] Others place meaning in how the text affects its reader. In other words, meaning is to be found not in the text itself or the author behind the text but how the reader

---

[7]Though the origin of this approach is disputed, its modern form can be traced to the formalist linguistic tradition pioneered by Noam Chomsky in the mid twentieth century. Chomsky believed in and taught an autonomous grammar inherent in all humans that followed universal linguistic principles, though he did not source "meaning" in these universal language principles. Chomsky's ideas, many of which were directly challenged, began multiple linguistic offshoots, including certain cognitive linguistics schools that do source meaning in texts apart from their author(s). A helpful survey of these movements is Stanley E. Porter, "Linguistic Schools," in *Linguistics and New Testament Greek: Key Issues in the Current Debate*, ed. by David Alan Black and Benjamin L. Merkle (Grand Rapids: Baker Academic, 2020), 11–36, esp. 20–35.

responds to the text.[8] Contrary to these approaches, I argue that *authorial intent* is the meaning of "meaning."

Every human who wishes to be understood by other humans *intends* or *wills* a meaning in their message.[9] All meaningful communication is predicated upon the speaker or writer *intending* to express their meaning to others. In his landmark study on interpretive theory, E. D. Hirsch made the following indisputable observation: "All forms of written interpretation and all interpretive goals that transcend private experience require that some author's meaning be both determinate and reproducible."[10] Hirsch's remark follows the triadic universal sequence of one person communicating to another: author—message—recipient. In written form, an author "determines" a meaning in their message, and the reader "reproduces" (interprets) that same meaning.

That this is the default position of all human communication serves to prove its legitimacy when

---

[8] Technically, this approach is termed "reader-response criticism." A useful introduction with critique can be found in Leland Ryken, "Literary Criticism and the Bible: Some Fallacies," in *Literary Interpretations of Biblical Narratives*, ed. by Kenneth R. R. Gross Louis, James S. Ackerman, and Thayer S. Warshaw (Nashville: Abingdon, 1974), 24–40.

[9] Incidentally, the same default rule applies even when humans communicate with nonhumans, such as animals. People desire (and expect) their pets to understand them!

[10] E. D. Hirsch, Jr., *Validity in Interpretation* (New Haven: Yale University Press, 1967), 27.

discerning "meaning" in biblical hermeneutics. There is a single intended meaning in every biblical passage, and that meaning is what the passage's author intended. Andreas Köstenberger and Richard Patterson put it this way:

> The rules of proper communication demand that we seek to understand the meaning the person communicating *intended to convey*. The text is not autonomous or a law unto itself, as if it existed apart from the author who willed and wrote it into being. It is an authorially shaped and designed product that requires careful and respectful interpretation.[11]

It seems unescapable, therefore, that even in the misplaced attempts above, it is impossible to sever the relationship between author and text—regardless of how the text is received. Even if an author wishes for their writing to be open-ended and interpreted any way the reader sees fit (a consequence to both approaches above), it was still *intended* that way to begin with.[12] As such, it is seems unescapable that "meaning" is ultimately sourced in the author's intention behind their text. Therefore, "meaning" should be defined as "authorial intent."

---

[11] Andreas J. Köstenberger and Richard D. Patterson, *For the Love of God's Word: An Introduction to Biblical Interpretation* (Grand Rapids: Kregel Academic, 2015), 17–18.

[12] I say this only to illustrate the point, not to imply in any way that Scripture was written with open-ended intentions.

Understanding Authorial Meaning Is Expected

Throughout the texts of Scripture, introductory formulae are used that strongly imply the reader is expected to understand the authorial meaning of those texts. One clear example is the 417 appearances of the expression "Thus says the LORD" throughout the Old Testament (OT) (e.g., Exod 4:22; 5:1; 7:17; 11:4; Josh 7:13; Judg 6:8; 2 Sam 7:5; 24:12; Isa 10:24; 28:16; 29:22; 31:4; 49:7; 56:1; Jer 2:2; 6:9; 10:2; 11:3, Zech 1:16; 8:23 et al.). It seems absurd to think that whatever follows such a strong interjection from Yahweh would be open for interpretation.

The use of introductory patterns in the New Testament (NT) likewise implies the reader is expected to understand Scripture's authorial meaning. Jesus's rhetorical question, "Have you not read?" enveloping the Gospels is one such example (e.g., Matt 12:5; 19:4; 22:31; Mark 12:10, 26; Luke 6:3; cf. John 12:14). Jesus's use of such a method to introduce an OT passage suggests He expected His audience to know the intended meaning of those passages, even if they had misunderstood it (He also apparently expected His audience to have actually "read" them!). Similarly, the rest of the NT abounds with introductory phrases like, "As it says in [the OT book or prophet]," "As Scripture says," "As it is written," "According to [an OT book or prophet]," and so on (see Acts 7:42; 15:15; Rom 4:6; 10:11, 20; Gal 3:6; 1 Thess 3:4; 2 Tim 3:8; Heb 3:2; 1 John 3:23; 2 John 6; Jude 7; Rev 10:7).

Paul and other NT writers appealed to OT Scripture this way to justify their own points and did so assuming their readers understood the intended meaning of those biblical passages. Otherwise, their appeals would be useless. Michael Vlach refers to this as a "consistent contextual use of the OT by NT writers' approach."[13] When the NT author quotes or appeals to the OT he does so *contextually*, maintaining the intended meaning of the OT author.[14]

Clearly, each of these ways the Bible declares a command or introduces a quote or allusion to other portions of Scripture signals an actual intended meaning in those texts—*and that both the original audience and reader today were/are expected to understand that intended meaning.* This means the Bible is not a free-for-all trinket open to any interpretation imaginable. It has an intended meaning that is actually expected to be understood. Therefore, the biblically literate Christian assumes that the biblical text really does faithfully represent the author's intended meaning behind

---

[13] Michael J. Vlach, *The Old in the New: Understanding How the New Testament Authors Quoted the Old Testament* (The Woodlands, TX: Kress Biblical Resources, 2021), 5–15.

[14] Ibid., 5.

those texts.[15] His or her goal is to "diligently discern"[16] the author's intended meaning expressed through their texts and rightly handle the word of truth (cf. 2 Tim 2:15).

Going back to the very first utterance in Scripture, "God said: 'Let there be light.'" The response immediately follows: "And there was light" (Gen 1:3). If God expects even inanimate elements to understand His intended meaning, how much more the Christian who is made in His image?

Upholding Authorial Meaning Is Ethical

There is an ethical dimension to how we read Scripture that often gets overlooked in discussions on hermeneutics: *to neglect the author's intention* (i.e., authorial meaning) *is to disrespect the author.* Everyone has experienced their words being taken out of context. It doesn't feel good. When a

---

[15] Some might argue that we can never truly know what a biblical author was actually *thinking* when he wrote his text. To an extent that is true as they are no longer present that we might ask them. However, we do possess their *written thoughts*, and that is the only matter of relevance for hermeneutics. We must assume, therefore, that their written thoughts faithfully represent their mental thoughts (at least the thoughts they sought to express).

[16] The verb Paul uses in 2 Timothy 2:15, σπουδάζω (*spoudazō*), is an emotionally charged word that can be translated, "be zealous, take pains, make every effort" (see its usage in Hebrews 4:11; 2 Peter 1:10, 15; 3:14). Moreover, it is fronting the clause which may signal an emphatic function in the verse.

speaker or writer communicates their message, it becomes an ethical violation if the listener or reader disregards the intended meaning and twists it to mean something else.

There is a helpful principle in Jesus's "golden rule" that resonates with an ethical interpretation of texts, namely, to respect an author's intended meaning. "So, whatever you wish that others would do to you, do also to them, for this is the Law and the Prophets" (Matt 7:12). Contextually, the "rule" is embedded in a sermon Jesus preached to Israel concerning the Kingdom (cf. v. 21) and summarizes the ethics of the OT in a most succinct fashion. However, Köstenberger and Patterson draw a helpful inference: "The 'golden rule' of interpretation requires that we extend the same courtesy to any text or author that we would want others to extend to our statements and writings."[17]

If Jesus's primary Jewish audience was expected to live their lives with virtue and integrity regulated by OT law, how much more would this be expected of Christians living under God's grace who are commanded to "do all things to glory of God" (1 Cor 10:31)? Surely this "all things" includes reading Scripture and respecting the meaning intended by its human authors. And, ultimately, it means respecting God who revealed Himself through Scripture's human authors.[18] Indeed, to read ethically is to read contextually even to the glory of God.

---

[17] Köstenberger and Patterson, *For the Love of God's Word*, 18.

[18] Cf. Ibid.

Context, Context, Context

My wife and I were driving the other day to one of our favorite spots with a nice path we like to walk. As we were waiting at a red light, I noticed a bumper sticker on the vehicle in front of us. The sticker had a Scripture verse with the words: Pray For Biden. With all the vitriol politicians usually receive, especially presidents, I was immediately cut to the heart by the biblical idea of praying for our country's leaders—and how often I neglect doing so. After all, Paul was clear that God is pleased when Christians pray for "kings and all those in high positions," which surely includes presidents in our day (1 Tim 2:1–4).

But I was confused by the Scripture verse on the bumper sticker. It wasn't Paul's admonition but a psalm that I couldn't mentally connect to the concept of praying for leaders. While waiting for the light to turn green, I clicked my Bible app to read the verse on the sticker, Psalm 109:8: "May his days be few; may another take his office!"

Needless to say, this psalm has nothing to do with praying for an American president to have a short office term. Psalm 109 is a strong imprecatory prayer for God's justice to try wicked men whose leader was unjustly accusing David with a barrage of lies and personal attacks. When David prayed "may his days be few," he meant it in the harshest way possible—the man's death. In case this was unclear, the next verse clarifies it: "May his children be fatherless, and his wife a widow!" (v. 10). The rest of the psalm gets even more brutal for the dead man's family.

Though such psalms can be difficult for a modern evangelical audience, it's important to understand that imprecation like that in Psalm 109 was a customary subgenre in Hebrew poetry (e.g., Psalm 5, 17, 59, 70, 83, 137, 140).

Imprecatory psalms are filled with dramatic rhetoric intended to exalt God's love and justice for those who trust in Him contrasted with requests for God's wrath and curses on those who hate Him or His delegates. In fact, part of the same verse on that bumper sticker was later quoted by Peter in the New Testament as he described wicked Judas who betrayed Jesus and committed suicide. Because he was now dead, another had to take his apostolic office (Acts 1:20). To exploit a passage that called for a man's death and continued trauma for his wife and children, as that bumper sticker did, not only highlights the driver's lack of biblical literacy but also severely trivializes God's holy words by discarding its original intent.

In the world of biblical hermeneutics—CONTEXT IS KING. To discern the authorial intent in any biblical passage is to understand it contextually. Contextual awareness is a game changer for many newer (and rusty) Bible readers. Context really is the number one essential element for a proper interpretation of Scripture's various literature.

Hermeneutical Cycles and Triads

Proof-texting is dangerous business. Too often, readers of Scripture disregard the surrounding context of a verse to make an immediate personal application of that verse. As my examples of Satan in Matthew 4:9 or the bumper sticker fiasco painfully illustrate, God did not reveal His will in isolated verses. The simple hermeneutical technique of reading a verse of Scripture in light of the greater whole is one surefire way to maintain a verse's context. Consider the figure below.

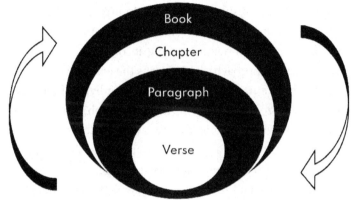

Fig. 3.1 Hermeneutical Cycle

We might label such a figure a *hermeneutical cycle.* The idea is that one's understanding of the whole is informed by the individual verse, and one's understanding of the individual verse is informed by the whole.[19] There is mild

---

[19] Some have referred to this idea as a hermeneutical "circle" or "spiral," but I believe "cycle" is the best metaphor to visualize *different layers* in the process of maintaining context. A hermeneutical circle can suggest an infinite wheel or merry-go-round without progress, while a hermeneutical spiral has been described with such elasticity, depending on its advocate, the concept has become quite muddied. See, for example, the

debate over starting points. Is it better to begin at the individual verse and work up through the cycles to reach the book level (bottom-up)? Or should one start at book level and filter down through the cycles and land on the verse (top-down)? Since the goal of both approaches is to ensure proper literary context for meaning, both methods are equally valid. In the end, applying either a top-down or bottom-up approach should result in the same interpretation as each level informs the other. That said, I generally prefer to begin with larger contexts before zeroing in on the smaller ones (the top-down approach). This means the entire book is first surveyed before narrowing down to the individual chapter, followed by zooming in on the paragraph, and finally analyzing the verse. Obviously, the reverse order is applied if one prefers to follow a bottom-up approach. Space limits elaboration, but a top-down approach is largely influenced by linguistic theory and discourse analysis that views meaning existing above the sentence level.[20] I agree with this in

---

differences of usage in J. I. Packer, "Biblical Authority, Hermeneutics, and Inerrancy," in *Jerusalem and Athens: Critical Discussions on the Theology and Apologetics of Cornelius Van Til*, ed. by E. R. Geehan (Philipsburg, NJ: P&R, 1980), 141–153, and Grant R. Osborne, *The Hermeneutical Spiral: A Comprehensive Introduction to Biblical Interpretation* (Downers Grove, IL: IVP Academic, 2006).

[20] A technical and insightful (and mammoth!) volume that applies this approach to each book of the New Testament is, *Discourse Analysis of the New Testament Writings,* ed. by Todd A. Scacewater (Dallas: Fontes, 2020).

principle, as it reinforces the point that the Bible was not revealed in isolated verses; each verse is embedded in a larger context.

Before a Christian can properly apply a text or biblical principle today, it is crucial they understand the situation in which it was first revealed. What were the surrounding cultural, political, or ecclesial issues occasioning the writing? Who was the original human author (or at best, the likely author), and who was the original audience? In what economy or dispensation was the text written or to which economy is it referring (e.g., law, grace, kingdom)? What type of literary genre is the text, and where does it sit in the overall canon of Scripture? How does one verse relate to another verse in a paragraph, and how does that paragraph relate to the book or letter as a whole? What are the theological themes that reveal God's character and His relationship to creation?

These are a smattering of questions that guide the biblically literate Christian into awareness and proficiency of Scripture *before* they apply what they read. For as Zuck wisely pointed out, "We must know the meaning of the Bible before we can know its message for today. We must understand the Bible's sense for then before we can see its significance for now."[21] Maintaining the text's context guards against the all-too-popular interpretive fallacy of reader-response, which looks to *self* for meaning. The biblically literate reader does not vainly ask, What does this text mean to *me*? Instead, they

---

[21] Zuck, *Basic Bible Interpretation*, 10.

take a step back and ask, What does this text mean to God, the original human author, and the original audience? Only then do they ask how (or if) they should apply it today. Undoubtedly, *context* is the most fundamental tool for the reader of Scripture to keep in mind.

Thus, when studying any passage of Scripture, the Christian is sure to respect the text's historical background and the grammar the author used to make sure we understand it in proper context. These three factors—history, literature, and theology—must be assessed judiciously if we are to attain a valid interpretation. A tried-and-true process that helps maintain the Bible's historical, literary, and theological contexts is to follow three steps in the order of the figure below: observation (historical background matters), interpretation (type of genre, syntax, word meanings), and then application (what it teaches about God and how we are supposed to respond). Such an order is exemplified in what has been termed the *hermeneutical triad*.[22]

---

[22] The term "hermeneutical triad" was coined and is best explained / applied by Andreas J. Köstenberger with Richard D. Patterson, *Invitation to Biblical Interpretation: Exploring the Hermeneutical Triad of History, Literature, and Theology,* 2nd ed. (Grand Rapids: Kregel Academic, 2020). It is from them that I borrow the geometric shape (triangle) with its progressive order—history, literature, and theology.

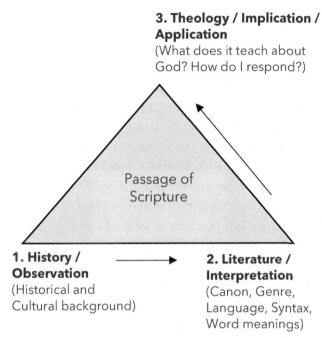

3. Theology / Implication / Application
(What does it teach about God? How do I respond?)

Passage of Scripture

1. History / Observation
(Historical and Cultural background)

2. Literature / Interpretation
(Canon, Genre, Language, Syntax, Word meanings)

Fig 3.2 Hermeneutical Triad

Scripture Progresses, Not Regresses

As a method of interpreting Scripture to gain awareness and proficiency, biblical hermeneutics can also be thought of in terms of *Bible study*. But a Bible study method need not entail some rigid, mechanistic process of steps. Its aim is not mechanical imitation. Rather, by developing in *method* we develop in *person*.[23] A person's hermeneutical method grows the reader's awareness of and proficiency in Scripture in order to understand God's revealed will. Obviously, this affects the person's life and how they live toward others.

While each individual writing of Scripture was not always produced in a strict linear progression (i.e., each book chronologically written in the exact order it appears in our Bibles), the overall canon of Scripture is certainly arranged in the way the two major Testaments were historically revealed: first, the Old Testament; second, the New Testament. This very arrangement suggests a proper method of Bible study will be one that is progressive or forward-looking.[24] Scripture progresses, not regresses. So should our method.

Like a house that is built upon a foundation before its walls are erected, the OT should be understood as providing the foundation for the NT. And, just like the walls, windows, or roof of a house do not repurpose or change its foundation, neither does the NT repurpose or change the meaning of the OT. Whatever the original intended meaning was in the OT, it was fully sufficient for its purposes and is never altered or canceled by the NT. Though the NT may supply additional information or draw fresh implications and analogies from

---

[23] Cf. Andreas J. Köstenberger and Richard Alan Fuhr Jr., *Inductive Bible Study: Observation, Interpretation, and Application through the Lenses of History, Literature, and Theology* (Nashville: B&H Academic, 2016), 44.

[24] See Ibid., 209–211; cf. "the progressive principle," 32–33.

an OT text (e.g., Matt 2:15; 1 Pet 1:10–11), the passing of time does not violate clearly stated referents, promises, and established meaning of the earlier revelation. Contrary to claims that Christians should "unhitch" the NT from the OT[25], the NT is only properly understood in the light of the OT. The OT can stand on its own and was even clear enough that Timothy found salvation in Christ through it (see 2 Timothy 3:15).[26] The Bible is not the Bible without both the OT and NT together.[27] Therefore, a correct hermeneutical (and theological) method of Bible study is one that reads the NT in *the light of the OT*, not the converse order. In this sense, "priority" (or starting point) must be given to the OT.[28]

---

[25] For example, Andy Stanley's recent best seller *Irresistible: Reclaiming the New that Jesus Unleashed from the World* (Grand Rapids: Zondervan, 2018) promotes "unhitching" the OT from Christianity.

[26] It is largely the OT that Paul had in mind when he explained that these ἱερὰ γράμματα (*hiera grammata*, "sacred writings") are able to make Timothy "wise for salvation through faith in Christ Jesus" (v. 15). That Paul also had in mind whatever NT Scriptures were completed by the time he wrote to Timothy is also likely. Cf. George W. Knight, *Commentary on the Pastoral Epistles*, NIGNT (Grand Rapids: Eerdmans, 1992), 448.

[27] See Mark S. Gignilliat, "Old Testament: How Did the New Testament Authors Use the Tanak," in *Understanding the Jewish Roots of Christianity: Biblical, Theological, and Historical Essays on the Relationship between Christianity and Judaism*, SSBT, ed., Gerald R. McDermott (Bellingham: Lexham Press, 2021), 5–17.

[28] This prioritizing order goes against many evangelical scholars who prefer to approach Scripture through the lens of the NT and draw theological conclusions by reading "backward" to the OT. But such an

The Clarity of Scripture and Consistent Hermeneutics

In addition to understanding the Bible in relation to its progressive revelation, a method that properly respects Scripture's context and discerns authorial meaning is one that maintains consistency. Indeed, clarity demands consistency.

When Genesis 1 uses "day" (*yôm*) for the creation week, consistency will view it denoting the same period of time as a "day" in man's weekly cycle (Exod 20:10–11; Deut 5:12–15). Consistency will also maintain a literal reading of the virgin conception of Jesus *as well as* His future reign over Israel, as one verse follows the other (Luke 1:31–32). Likewise, consistency will not interpret "Israel" as a nation in Romans 11:25 while interpreting "Israel" as something different in the very next verse (v. 26). While context is the ultimate factor in determining a word's meaning—since words by themselves have a range of meaning—consistency helps maintain context.

Consistency is the key, and a reliable system of interpretation is one that not only approaches the Scriptures with belief in its divine origin but is also, as Elliot Johnson argues, "developed through a system of consistent, reasoned

---

order impinges on the doctrine of progressive revelation and risks devaluing the OT's sufficiency, especially for saints living before NT revelation.

principles."[29] Such an approach is demanded by the *perspicuity*, or clarity, of Scripture. That is to say, claiming the Bible is clear or understandable is to depend on a consistent method of interpretation that justifies the claim. While there will always be passages in Scripture that are clearer than others, a consistent interpretive method will guard the Bible reader from arbitrarily choosing different readings whenever challenged.

The Most Consistent Hermeneutical Method

As I see it, the most consistent biblical hermeneutic that is founded on reasoned principles is the *literal method*. The technical term is the *literal, grammatical-historical* hermeneutical method. Non-technical ways to explain it are the plain sense, clear sense, natural sense (etc.) of Scripture. Some, like Mark Snoeberger, prefer the term *originalist* to describe this method of interpretation as it guards the *original intentions* of a given document's author, binding its authorial intention.[30] Regardless of the exact term used, this consistent method is built on the idea that the Bible is not obscure, needing a supposed-prophet, pope, or elected

---

[29] Johnson, *Expository Hermeneutics*, 21.

[30] Mark A. Snoeberger, "Traditional Dispensationalism," in *Covenantal and Dispensational Theologies: Four Views on the Continuity of Scripture*, ed. by Brent E. Parker and Richard J. Lucas (Downers Grove: IVP Academic, 2022), 153.

committee to understand it.[31] Rather, the Bible's perspicuity (clarity) lends itself quite naturally to a literal interpretation of Scripture.[32]

The literal method of interpretation is built around two main components: grammar and history (hence, *grammatical-historical*). For each passage examined, both the *grammar of the text* (semantics and syntax) and the *facts of history* (historical context and factual historical hindsight) are surveyed at the discourse and sentence level. From these two components follows application or, in the broader sense, *theology*. With a keen eye toward the text's history, literature, and theology filtered through the process of observation, interpretation, and application, the passage's grammar and history are exegeted in order to reach one main goal: *the Author/author's single-intended meaning*. This literal, grammatical-historical method should be consistently

---

[31] By "elected committees," I am not referring to *translation committees* viz., qualified language experts that lend their skills in translating the Bible into a target language. Such teams are invaluable for Bible translation.

[32] See Jeremiah Mutie, "Neither Woodenly-Literal nor Allegorical: The Dispensationalist Legacy of the Reformers' Doctrine of *Sola Scriptura*," in *Forged from Reformation: How Dispensational Thought Advances the Reformed Legacy* (El Cajon: SCS Press, 2017), 353–380, esp. 357–358.

applied from Genesis to Revelation because the goal is always the same—discerning the single-intended meaning.[33]

Fig 3.3 The Literal, Grammatical-Historical Method.

The concept of single intention does not violate the dual authorship of Scripture—that is, the Bible being written by both God and man. As Robert Stein put it, "The divine meaning of the biblical text *is* the conscious willed meaning of God's inspired prophets and apostles."[34] Moreover, Rolland McCune argued in his defense of "the unitary authorship of Scripture," that every proposition of Scripture carries a singular attention *despite* its dual authorship by virtue of the miracle of inspiration.[35] The production of the

---

[33] A notable work defending single-intended authorial meaning is Robert L. Thomas, *Evangelical Hermeneutics: The New Versus the Old* (Grand Rapids: Kregel Academic, 2003). Thomas did overstate his case at times and maintained (an unfortunate) bias against general linguistics. Nevertheless, his work champions the single-meaning principle better than most.

[34] Robert H. Stein, *A Basic Guide to Interpreting the Bible: Playing by the Rules* (Grand Rapids: Baker, 2001), 28.

[35] Rolland D. McCune, "What Is Literal Interpretation of Scripture?" paper presented at the Mid-America Conference of Preaching at Detroit

original Scriptures is itself a miracle, safeguarding God's intent expressed through each biblical writer's personality for a combined single-intended authorial meaning. This is the case whether reading the Bible's poetry, like the Psalms with its figures of speech, or didactic ("teaching") literature like the NT epistles. When the passage's grammar and history are examined within their contexts, its authorial meaning is discovered.

Also, key is that while the passage may have far reaching *significance* allowing for multiple applications, the *meaning* of the text is fixed and singular. This is a critical distinction. As defined earlier, meaning is equated with authorial intent. A text's significance, however, involves both its implication and application.

If someone so affected by the Great Commission passage of Matthew 28 was to state it *meant* they were to become a missionary in Uganda, what they are really describing is the passage's *significance* as it relates to their unique calling. The text in Matthew actually *means* that the eleven disciples were granted authority by Jesus to make disciples of all the nations in the name of the triune Godhead, backed by the continuing presence of Christ in all their efforts (vv. 18–20). Its *significance* is further reaching, extending past merely the eleven remaining disciples to individual Christians of every age and in every place (like the missionary feeling led to Uganda). One may apply the same

Baptist Theological Seminary (Oct 19–20, 2000), 157–162, quoted in Mark A. Snoeberger, "Traditional Dispensationalism," 154n15.

passage in their calling to pastor a local church. Another may apply it in their calling to be a military chaplain. And still another may apply it in their personal evangelism and one-on-one discipleship in their neighborhood. In any case, these applications comprise the *significance* of Matthew 28:18–20 while the *meaning* of the text is firm and unalterable. In other words—one meaning, various applications.

Concept	Definition
Meaning ⟶	Authorial Intent
Significance ⟶	Implication and Application

Fig 3.4 Meaning vs. Significance

However, even implications and applications are not completely detached from the author's single intent. For instance, though David snuck up to Saul and cut off a piece of his robe while Saul was "relieving himself" (1 Sam 24:1–7), it is wrong to think this implies we should attack people in restrooms! Clearly, any significance a text may have must first have its basis in an accurate interpretation of that text—since one can easily misapply or draw a wrong implication from it.[36] This recalls the importance of the sequence of steps described earlier in exegeting a text's history, literature, and theology *through* observation, interpretation, and finally application (See Figure 3.5).

---

[36] See Köstenberger and Fuhr, *Inductive Bible Study*, 41; cf. Vlach, *The Old in the New*, 5

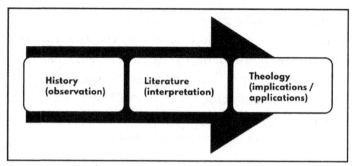

Fig 3.5 Sequential Steps

So, a consistent (evangelical) hermeneutical approach will demand that historical and literary contexts be kept at the fore in every passage explored, and that the interpreter will do so assuming the Scripture's full inspiration and ultimate origin from God.[37] The principle of *sola Scriptura* teaches that God's Word alone has ultimate authority over the Christian's life. A corollary principle is Scripture's omnisufficiency; that is, Scripture is entirely sufficient for application. As Ken Casillas observed, "Application is the only way the Bible can exercise its authority over our lives. Similarly, application is the only way the Bible can be sufficient for our lives."[38] In other words, a Bible that is truly authoritative and all-sufficient will be demonstrated by its application. Such ideas, while not exclusive to the model, are

---

[37] See the Appendices for *The Chicago Statement on Biblical Inerrancy* and how this relates to the Bible's inspiration.

[38] Ken Casillas, *Beyond Chapter and Verse: The Theology and Practice of Biblical Application* (Eugene, OR: Wipf & Stock, 2018), 152.

most consistently upheld in the literal, grammatical-historical method of hermeneutics.

Applying What's Been Said: Two Examples

After all that has been said, I think it is helpful to wrap up by briefly applying the hermeneutical principles above to two examples in Scripture often taken out of context. Bearing in mind that biblical hermeneutics is both "science" and "art," this is merely my attempt at applying the principles stated throughout this chapter. These principles provide guide rails, but, in the end, each interpreter is subject to their own skill, knowledge, and—ultimately—dependence on the Holy Spirit as they engage in biblical hermeneutics (1 Cor 2:10–16; cf. 1 John 2:27).

By reading these verses through the lenses of history, literature, and theology and applying a literal, grammatical-historical hermeneutic, several observations are made that yield what I believe to be a correct interpretation and application.

Jeremiah 29:11

"For I know the plans I have for you, declares the Lord, plans for welfare and not for evil, to give you a future and a hope."

1. *Historically*, Jeremiah was called by Yahweh primarily to declare coming judgments on God's people as well as surrounding nations. During the prophet's day, Israel, which was split in two, had violated the Mosaic covenant, and had already suffered through Assyrian invasions and captivities in the north (11:10–11). Jeremiah had warned Judah in the south of coming Babylonian oppression and captivity due to their rampant idolatry, but it went ignored. By the time of chapter 29, the warnings had come to fruition with Judah and its temple destroyed and the Jews taken as slaves by Nebuchadnezzar. Verse 11 is then given by Yahweh through the prophet Jeremiah to surviving Israelites of the Babylonian captivity (v. 1). It communicates hope amid disaster as Yahweh would not forget His people with promises of restoration for national Israel in the latter days (30:3).

2. As for the *literature* of the book, its placement in the Protestant canon is obviously OT as it is nestled between the major prophets of Isaiah through Daniel—all of which were written primarily to Israelites. Jeremiah seems to be dominated by historical-narrative prose with large elements of prophecy. The impressive amount of consecutive preterite verb forms customary to narrative genre (i.e., the conjunction "and" + imperfect verb) move the story along sequentially, distinguishing the book from Hebrew poetry (though poetic sections certainly exist in Jeremiah). The first four verses of chapter 29 describe historically the events that led to this "letter" (or

"message" or "book") Jeremiah wrote, which contains verse 11. This letter of prophecy was intended for surviving slaves from Judah in Babylon (note the plural "you"), which include instructions from Yahweh on how to faithfully reside in their current situation—even seeking the welfare of their captors (v. 7). Immediately following verse 11 is a lengthy prophecy of curses upon Israel—including sword, famine, and pestilence—due to them listening to false prophets while in Babylon (vv. 15–23). Destructive curses also fall on the false prophets themselves (vv. 21–24). In the middle of captivity, death, and destruction for the Israelites stands verse 11, signaling a beacon of hope as Yahweh will not forget His people. He prophesied their eventual national restoration, later solidified in the New Covenant passage in chapter 31.

3. The *theology* of the passage is rich. It should be recalled that verse 11 was not given in isolation, nor to individuals, but as part of a package of curses and blessings on corporate Israel for their breaking of the covenant (cf. Deut 5). They had allowed pagan nations and geopolitical pressures to swerve them from faithfulness to the Law into rampant idolatry and wickedness. God does not tolerate such rebellion from His people, and He acted on His promises of captivity since they did not repent. Yet even in the midst of horror and suffering, Yahweh remained faithful to His promises to Israel, which originated with His call to Abraham (Gen

12:1–3). They will be a nation that blesses the world (see 31:31–34), most explicitly through the Jewish Messiah who would be born according to the very tribe that was carried away into Babylon.

⇒ **The single-intended meaning of Jeremiah 29:11:** God will one day restore national Israel for their good and His glory when they seek Him with all their heart and call upon Him in repentance.

⇒ **Implication / Application:** Trust that if the Lord does not forget His promises to Israel, He will not forget His promises to the church. Repentance should characterize the believer's life, especially in times of distress.

Philippians 4:13

"I can do all things through Him who strengthens me."

1. The *historical* context of the verse places the Apostle Paul in Roman imprisonment, awaiting his appeals made to Caesar, most likely Nero, in the early to mid-60s AD (1:7). Accompanied by Timothy (1:1), he wrote to the church at Philippi to thank them for their support of his ministry which was likely financial in nature (1:4–5; 4:14–18). By this time, Paul had completed three difficult missions throughout the Mediterranean, which included beatings, stonings, and shipwrecks, along with various

imprisonments in Israel for preaching the gospel (see Acts 13–27; cf. 20:23–24). Now under house arrest in Rome, Paul wrote to the Philippians along with letters to the churches at Ephesus and Colossae and to his friend Philemon.

2. The *literature* of Philippians is clearly *epistle* (Greek for "letter") signified by the customary salutations for which Paul is known (1:1–2 and 4:21–23). Situated in the NT canon, the letter is considered one of Paul's undisputed Prison Epistles, written to a predominately gentile church. Verse 13 appears within the final unit of thought that Paul gives to the Philippian church (vv. 10–20) before his concluding greetings (vv. 21–23). The word group for "joy" is prominent throughout the epistle (1:4, 18, 25; 2:2, 17, 28–29; 3:1; 4:1), the final appearance of which initiates this unit with Paul "rejoicing" in response to the Philippian Christians' care and concern for him (v. 10). Verse 14 contains Paul's gratitude for the Philippians sharing in his "trouble," a word elsewhere used of severe "affliction" and "tribulation" (see John 16:33). Sandwiched between Paul's joy for their concern in verse 10 and reminder of his own trouble in verse 14 is his description of the ebb and flow of ministry, ranging from prosperity to deprivation (vv. 11–12). It is in this context that verse 13 begins with an emphatic plural adjective "all [things]" to describe Paul's ministry affairs of highs and lows. The verse continues with a rare first-person verb "I am strong" and ends with a present participle

"strengthening." Holding these words together is the prepositional phrase "in Him," which locates Paul's strength in God alone.

3. *Theologically*, the message is clear. No matter what hardship or relief Paul experienced while preaching the gospel and planting churches, he learned contentment through it all by relying on God's strength. Suffering and trials were not the exception but the expectation for Paul's ministry. While God certainly provided Paul "abundance" (or more than enough) at times, He also allowed Paul to endure extreme hardship. The "secret" for Paul's ministry success was being content in any situation and relying on God's strength to see him through it (vv. 12–13). Such a lesson is invaluable for Christians in any context, especially those serving in gospel ministry. God supplies the supernatural power that believers need to serve Him in whatever situation He has ordained for them.

⇒ **The single-intended meaning of Philippians 4:13:** Whether distress or prosperity confronted the apostle Paul during his ministry, he was able to accomplish his tasks faithfully through the power and strength God supplied, resulting in personal contentment.

⇒ **Implication / Application:** Christian ministry requires a divine power which is available only in God and accessible for those relying on Him for their needs. All Christians, especially pastors and missionaries, should expect difficult times in gospel ministry, but Christ supplies them the strength needed to joyfully serve Him in any circumstance.

Summation

By applying a system of consistent, reasoned principles, these passages reveal an authorial meaning not often framed on walls or embroidered on boxing trunks. Though both verses make for decorative artwork, such artwork generally violates their historical, literary, and theological contexts. Jeremiah 29:11 is set within a context of both curses and blessings for the nation of Israel. Philippians 4:13 is set within a context of ministry difficulties for a Christian leader in prison. By applying literal hermeneutics, the message becomes clear for both. *Even through horrific national tragedy, God will one day restore Israel. Even through personal trauma, God grants Christians strength of contentment.* A literal, grammatical-historical approach ensures the author's intended meaning is respected.

No *Sui Generis* Theology

By saying that "everything boils down to hermeneutics,"[39] what I mean is that at the root level of anyone's doctrine or theology lies an interpretation. There are no exceptions. No one invents a doctrine *sui generis*, completely unique to itself. Hermeneutics, theology, and authority are intertwined. On the far end, the cults examined in Chapter 1 testify to this fact as do orthodox traditions on the other end.

As J. I. Packer expressed, "Every hermeneutic implies a theology, just as every theology involves a hermeneutic, so that where a false hermeneutic operates the Bible will not in fact have authority, whatever is claimed to the contrary."[40] All readers of Scripture base their doctrinal conclusions on a certain understanding of Scripture. Unmistakably, hermeneutics is an essential tool—rather *the* essential tool—which leads to one's theology. And correct hermeneutics is essential for correct theology.

As I have argued in this chapter, a consistent, literal hermeneutic is the best method for Christians to gain awareness and proficiency in Scripture in order to understand God's revealed will. With a view toward the Bible's history, literature, and theology, Scripture's grammatical and historical contexts are maintained and

---

[39] This is a saying I often use in my teaching at the college and seminary levels.

[40] Packer, "Biblical Authority, Hermeneutics, and Inerrancy," 141.

reproduce the single, authorial-intended meaning. Only then can responsible application follow.

CONCLUSION

Scripture Cannot Be Broken

Evangelical Christians rightly make much of the principle *sola Scriptura*, recovered during the Protestant Reformation in the sixteenth century. Instead of the pope or shifting tides of tradition having ultimate authority over the Christian life, the courageous Reformers defended Scripture as having that role. It was "Scripture alone" that reigned supreme as the final arbiter of truth. Going back-to-the-Bible as they did, the Reformers noticed Scripture's self-authenticating claims that simply refused to be subsumed by any human institution. They saw that Jesus Himself stunned crowds by grounding ultimate truth in God's Word. "Scripture cannot be broken" (John 10:35), He contended, and prayed to the Father, "Sanctify them in the truth; *your word is truth*" (17:17, emphasis added).

It seems unbelievable that so-called Christian institutions would persecute and murder other Christians for studying the Bible in the original languages and working tirelessly to translate them into the language of the common people. But that's exactly what happened. These diligent readers of God's truth came to understand the Bible as an authority higher than the Roman Catholic Church or any other state institution. They argued that as Spirit-indwelt priests before God, Christians are bound by Scripture—*Scripture alone*—and not shackled to conflicting church councils, kings, or corrupt clergy.[1] Many of them were rewarded for their convictions with torture and death—like William Tyndale, the first person to translate the original Hebrew and Greek Scriptures into the English language. In 1536, Tyndale was strangled and burned for his efforts.[2] Yet his presence is felt in virtually every English translation of the Bible since. Truly, Scripture cannot be broken.

As I stated at the outset, this brief book is a very modest attempt at connecting church ministry and scholarship on the essential subject of biblical literacy. It was guided by the idea that it is not only *possible* for Christians to understand the Bible but, in large measure, they are *expected* to understand it. As Chapter 2 pointed out, every Christian reader of Scripture is able to gain awareness and proficiency

---

[1] This was Martin Luther's contention against what he called the "Romanist walls" in his "An Open Letter to the Christian Nobility of the German Nation Concerning the Reform of the Christian Estate" published in 1520 which became his Reformation manifesto. For a more detailed analysis, see my essay, "Luther Meets Darby: The Reformation Legacy of Ecclesiastical Independence," in *Forged from Reformation*, 109–144.

[2] A very accessible and enjoyable volume on Tyndale's life is, Steven J. Lawson, *The Daring Mission of William Tyndale* (Sanford, FL: Reformation Trust, 2015). A more erudite and comprehensive biography that pays particular homage to Tyndale as the father of modern English is, David Daniell, *William Tyndale: A Biography* (New Haven: Yale University Press, 2001).

in their knowledge of the Bible. Expertise is not the goal. Increasing in one's *awareness* of God by reading through the Scriptures while gaining *proficiency* in understanding Scripture's meaning is the goal. This involves recognizing the Bible's various historical contexts and literary genres and, from there, discerning the intended authorial meaning expressed through those contexts. Chapter 3 furthered the discussion by highlighting that only after observing cultural and historical backgrounds and interpreting the Scripture's meaning does modern-day application then follow. If the horrific cultists surveyed in Chapter 1 had understood the importance of Scripture's historical, literary, and theological contexts for accurate meaning and proper application, they would not be considered cultists today. The same can be said of the prosperity charlatans who likewise highjack Scripture for greedy gain. Accurate comprehension of the Bible is predicated on a consistent hermeneutical method, which both groups horrendously lack[ed]. But, as clarified in Chapter 2, sound hermeneutics is not all that is required. Indeed, only a Spirit-filled regenerate believer in Jesus Christ can ultimately understand *and* submit to Scripture.

Of course, some parts of the Bible will remain a mystery, and that's okay. Our job is not to demand that every passage of Scripture answer every question we have of it. Rather, it is safe to assume that if God revealed Himself in the Bible (which He did), then He would want us to understand the overall message of the Bible. The message that God is glorified throughout all of creation history and that He intended to reveal His thoughts to mankind roars thunderously throughout Scripture. It's hard for the Christian not to hear it. There are no interpretive challenges to the basic biblical idea that sin has separated us from God and that reconciliation is possible only through His Son, Jesus Christ. Such a clear message permeates the Scriptures.

Though much more can be said on what it means to be biblically literate, I hope this book at least whetted the appetite for you to *want* to read the Bible. There was, and is, no greater thrill in my own life than being floored by the wisdom of God and the brilliance of the men contained in the Scriptures. Whenever I think I "got it," something else jumps off the page that I failed to consider. It could be something as small as a conjunction or tense of a verb in Paul's letters or a pronoun I overlooked in Jesus's discourses in John. I still get blown away by Moses's grand sweeps of creation history moving forward through dispensations in time along with various covenants, as well as David's exploding portraits of God's character in the Psalms. Recently I taught through Hebrews and was once again enamored by the fact that it's the only NT writing that is entirely anonymous. Excitement filled the discussion as we considered the various potential candidates from church history who might have written this amazing letter (personally, I lean toward Apollos!). Is it even a letter? Maybe it's a book or sermon. If a sermon, it's an actual inspired homily—what a template for preachers. And don't get me started on John! As I became more familiar with his writing style, it one day dawned on me that he's the only NT writer to give us multiple, in fact, *four* distinct literary genres: Gospel (John), epistle (2, 3 John), homily (1 John), and prophecy (Revelation). What an incredible array of genius for someone the religionists mistook as "illiterate and common" (Acts 4:13)! There really is nothing incidental in Scripture.

Those who know me know I can talk about this all day. The Bible never gets old. And it shouldn't for you either. It is filled with God's glory and human adventure. Far too many Christians have given (and continue to give) their lives to make sure we have it. Let us never become so familiar with it that we fail to see our need for it. My prayer is that as you apply the *why*, *what*, and *how* of biblical literacy explained in this book, you will be excited to learn the Scriptures afresh—and the living God revealed through them—and achieve biblical literacy.

APPENDICES

AN INTRODUCTION TO THE CHICAGO
STATEMENT

The following confessional statement was produced in October 1978 by the International Council on Biblical Inerrancy. Drafted by the largest and broadest group of conservative Protestant pastors and scholars to ever assemble up to that point for a shared theological cause, the Chicago Statement on Biblical Inerrancy is considered a landmark document for evangelical belief on the inspiration and authority of Scripture. One of its most prominent signers, J. I. Packer, declared, "The fact is that inerrancy, as we have defined it, is not merely a truth, but an essential and fundamental truth. Surrender it, and neither the authority of the Bible nor the knowledge of Jesus Christ, and God's grace in him, can remain intact."[1]

While the original document is housed in the Dallas Theological Seminary Archives, the version below was published in the *Journal of the Evangelical Theological Society* 21, no. 4 (Dec 1978): 289–296, almost immediately after the original draft was completed. It is reprinted here in its entirety with permission.

---

[1] Packer, "Biblical Authority, Hermeneutics, and Inerrancy," 153.

THE CHICAGO STATEMENT ON BIBLICAL

INERRANCY

Preface

The authority of Scripture is a key issue for the Christian Church in this and every age. Those who profess faith in Jesus Christ as Lord and Savior are called to show the reality of their discipleship by humbly and faithfully obeying God's written Word. To stray from Scripture in faith or conduct is disloyalty to our Master. Recognition of the total truth and trustworthiness of Holy Scripture is essential to a full grasp and adequate confession of its authority.[1]

The following Statement affirms this inerrancy of Scripture afresh, making clear our understanding of it and warning against its denial. We are persuaded that to deny it is to set aside the witness of Jesus Christ and of the Holy Spirit and to refuse that submission to the claims of God's own Word that marks true Christian faith. We see it as our timely duty to make this affirmation in the face of current lapses

---

[1] The International Council on Biblical Inerrancy, headquartered in Oakland, California, selected a draft committee from its membership to produce this statement on Biblical inerrancy in a three-day series of marathon sessions at the Hyatt Regency O'Hare, October 26–28, 1978.

from the truth of inerrancy among our fellow Christians and misunderstanding of this doctrine in the world at large.

This Statement consists of three parts: A Summary Statement, Articles of Affirmation and Denial, and an accompanying Exposition. It has been prepared in the course of a three-day consultation in Chicago. Those who have signed the Summary Statement and the Articles wish to affirm their own conviction as to the inerrancy of Scripture and to encourage and challenge one another and all Christians to growing appreciation and understanding of this doctrine. We acknowledge the limitations of a document prepared in a brief, intensive conference and do not propose that this Statement be given creedal weight. Yet we rejoice in the deepening of our own convictions through our discussions together, and we pray that the Statement we have signed may be used to the glory of our God toward a new reformation of the Church in its faith, life and mission.

We offer this Statement in a spirit, not of contention, but of humility and love, which we purpose by God's grace to maintain in any future dialogue arising out of what we have said. We gladly acknowledge that many who deny the inerrancy of Scripture do not display the consequences of this denial in the rest of their belief and behavior, and we are conscious that we who confess this doctrine often deny it in life by failing to bring our thoughts and deeds, our traditions and habits, into true subjection to the divine Word.

We invite response to this Statement from any who see reason to amend its affirmations about Scripture by the light of Scripture itself, under whose infallible authority we stand as we speak. We claim no personal infallibility for the witness we bear, and for any help that enables us to strengthen this testimony to God's Word we shall be grateful.

I. SUMMARY STATEMENT

1. God, who is Himself Truth and speaks truth only, has inspired Holy Scripture in order thereby to reveal Himself to lost mankind through Jesus Christ as Creator and Lord, Redeemer and Judge. Holy Scripture is God's witness to Himself.

2. Holy Scripture, being God's own Word, written by men prepared and superintended by His Spirit, is of infallible divine authority in all matters upon which it touches: It is to be believed, as God's instruction, in all that it affirms; obeyed, as God's command, in all that it requires; embraced, as God's pledge, in all that it promises.

3. The Holy Spirit, Scripture's divine Author, both authenticates it to us by His inward witness and opens our minds to understand its meaning.

4. Being wholly and verbally God-given, Scripture is without error or fault in all its teaching, no less in what it states about God's acts in creation, about the events of world history, and about its own literary origins under God, than in its witness to God's saving grace in individual lives.

5. The authority of Scripture is inescapably impaired if this total divine inerrancy is in any way limited or

disregarded, or made relative to a view of truth contrary to the Bible's own; and such lapses bring serious loss to both the individual and the Church.

II. ARTICLES OF AFFIRMATION AND DENIAL

Article I.

We affirm that the Holy Scriptures are to be received as the authoritative Word of God.

We deny that the Scriptures receive their authority from the Church, tradition, or any other human source.

Article II.

We affirm that the Scriptures are the supreme written norm by which God binds the conscience, and that the authority of the Church is subordinate to that of Scripture.

We deny that Church creeds, councils, or declarations have authority greater than or equal to the authority of the Bible.

Article III.

We affirm that the written Word in its entirety is revelation given by God.

We deny that the Bible is merely a witness to revelation, or only becomes revelation in encounter, or depends on the responses of men for its validity.

Article IV.

We affirm that God who made mankind in His image has used language as a means of revelation.

We deny that human language is so limited by our creatureliness that it is rendered inadequate as a vehicle for divine revelation. We further deny that the corruption of human culture and language through sin has thwarted God's work of inspiration.

Article V.

We affirm that God's revelation in the Holy Scriptures was progressive.

We deny that later revelation, which may fulfill earlier revelation, ever corrects or contradicts it. We further deny that any normative revelation has been given since the completion of the New Testament writings.

Article VI.

We affirm that the whole of Scripture and all its parts, down to the very words of the original, were given by divine inspiration.

We deny that the inspiration of Scripture can rightly be affirmed of the whole without the parts, or of some parts but not the whole.

Article VII.

We affirm that inspiration was the work in which God by His Spirit, through human writers, gave us His Word. The origin of Scripture is divine. The mode of divine inspiration remains largely a mystery to us.

We deny that inspiration can be reduced to human insight, or to heightened states of consciousness of any kind.

Article VIII.

We affirm that God in His work of inspiration utilized the distinctive personalities and literary styles of the writers whom He had chosen and prepared.

We deny that God, in causing these writers to use the very words that He chose, overrode their personalities.

Article IX.

We affirm that inspiration, though not conferring omniscience, guaranteed true and trustworthy utterance on all matters of which the Biblical authors were moved to speak and write.

We deny that the finitude or fallenness of these writers, by necessity or otherwise, introduced distortion or falsehood into God's Word.

Article X.

We affirm that inspiration, strictly speaking, applies only to the autographic text of Scripture, which in the providence of God can be ascertained from available manuscripts with great accuracy. We further affirm that copies and translations of Scripture are the Word of God to the extent that they faithfully represent the original.

We deny that any essential element of the Christian faith is affected by the absence of the autographs. We further deny that this absence renders the assertion of Biblical inerrancy invalid or irrelevant.

Article XI.

We affirm that Scripture, having been given by divine inspiration, is infallible, so that, far from misleading us, it is true and reliable in all the matters it addresses.

We deny that it is possible for the Bible to be at the same time infallible and errant in its assertions. Infallibility and inerrancy may be distinguished but not separated.

Article XII.

We affirm that Scripture in its entirety is inerrant, being free from all falsehood, fraud, or deceit.

We deny that Biblical infallibility and inerrancy are limited to spiritual, religious, or redemptive themes, exclusive of assertions in the fields of history and science. We further deny that scientific hypotheses about earth history may properly be used to overturn the teaching of Scripture on creation and the flood.

Article XIII.

We affirm the propriety of using inerrancy as a theological term with reference to the complete truthfulness of Scripture.

We deny that it is proper to evaluate Scripture according to standards of truth and error that are alien to its usage or purpose. We further deny that inerrancy is negated by Biblical phenomena such as a lack of modern technical precision, irregularities of grammar or spelling, observational descriptions of nature, the reporting of falsehoods, the use of hyperbole and round numbers, the topical arrangement of material, varient [*sic*] selections of material in parallel accounts, or the use of free citations.

Article XIV.

We affirm the unity and internal consistency of Scripture.

We deny that alleged errors and discrepancies that have not yet been resolved vitiate the truth claims of the Bible.

Article XV.

We affirm that the doctrine of inerrancy is grounded in the teaching of the Bible about inspiration.

We deny that Jesus' teaching about Scripture may be dismissed by appeals to accommodation or to any natural limitation of His humanity.

Article XVI.

We affirm that the doctrine of inerrancy has been integral to the Church's faith throughout its history.

We deny that inerrancy is a doctrine invented by scholastic Protestantism, or is a reactionary position postulated in response to negative higher criticism.

Article XVII.

We affirm that the Holy Spirit bears witness to the Scriptures, assuring believers of the truthfulness of God's written Word.

We deny that this witness of the Holy Spirit operates in isolation from or against Scripture.

Article XVIII.

We affirm that the text of Scripture is to be interpreted by grammatico-historical exegesis, taking account of its literary forms and devices, and that Scripture is to interpret Scripture.

We deny the legitimacy of any treatment of the text or quest for sources lying behind it that leads to relativizing, dehistoricizing, or discounting its teaching, or rejecting its claims to authorship.

Article XIX.

We affirm that a confession of the full authority, infallibility and inerrancy of Scripture is vital to a sound understanding of the whole of the Christian faith. We further affirm that such confession should lead to increasing conformity to the image of Christ.

We deny that such confession is necessary for salvation. However, we further deny that inerrancy can be rejected without grave consequences, both to the individual and to the Church.

III. EXPOSITION

Our understanding of the doctrine of inerrancy must be set in the context of the broader teachings of Scripture concerning itself. This exposition gives an account of the outline of doctrine from which our Summary Statement and Articles are drawn.

A. Creation, Revelation and Inspiration

The Triune God, who formed all things by His creative utterances and governs all things by His Word of decree, made mankind in His own image for a life of communion with Himself, on the model of the eternal fellowship of loving communication within the Godhead. As God's image-bearer, man was to hear God's Word addressed to him and to respond in the joy of adoring obedience. Over and above God's self-disclosure in the created order and the sequence of events within it, human beings from Adam on have received verbal messages from Him, either directly, as stated in Scripture, or indirectly in the form of part or all of Scripture itself.

When Adam fell, the Creator did not abandon mankind to final judgment but promised salvation and began to reveal Himself as Redeemer in a sequence of historical events centering on Abraham's family and culminating in the life, death, resurrection, present heavenly ministry and promised return of Jesus Christ. Within this frame God has from time to time spoken specific words of judgment and mercy, promise and command, to sinful human beings, so drawing them into a covenant relation of mutual commitment between Him and them in which He blesses them with gifts of grace and they bless Him in responsive adoration. Moses, whom God used as mediator to carry His words to His people at the time of the exodus, stands at the head of a long line of prophets in whose mouths and writings God put His words for delivery to Israel. God's purpose in this succession of messages was to maintain His covenant by causing His people to know His name—that is, His nature—and His will both of precept and purpose in the present and for the future. This line of prophetic spokesmen from God came to completion in Jesus Christ, God's incarnate Word, who was Himself a prophet—more than a prophet, but not less—and in the apostles and prophets of the first Christian generation. When God's final and climactic message, His word to the world concerning Jesus Christ, had been spoken and elucidated by those in the apostolic circle, the sequence of revealed messages ceased. Henceforth the Church was to live and know God by what He had already said, and said for all time.

At Sinai God wrote the terms of His covenant on tablets of stone as His enduring witness and for lasting accessibility, and throughout the period of prophetic and apostolic revelation He prompted men to write the messages given to and through them, along with celebratory records of His dealings with His people, plus moral reflections on covenant life and forms of praise and prayer for covenant mercy. The theological reality of inspiration in the producing of Biblical documents corresponds to that of spoken prophecies: Although the human writers' personalities were expressed in what they wrote, the words were divinely constituted. Thus what Scripture says, God says; its authority is His authority, for He is its ultimate Author, having given it through the minds and words of chosen and prepared men who in freedom and faithfulness "spoke from God as they were carried along by the Holy Spirit" (1 Pet 1:21). Holy Scripture must be acknowledged as the Word of God by virtue of its divine origin.

B. Authority: Christ and the Bible

Jesus Christ, the Son of God who is the Word made flesh, our Prophet, Priest and King, is the ultimate Mediator of God's communication to man, as He is of all God's gifts of grace. The revelation He gave was more than verbal; He revealed the Father by His presence and His deeds as well. Yet His words were crucially important; for He was God, He spoke from the Father, and His words will judge all men at the last day.

As the prophesied Messiah, Jesus Christ is the central theme of Scripture. The Old Testament looked ahead to Him; the New Testament looks back to His first coming and on to His second. Canonical Scripture is the divinely inspired and therefore normative witness to Christ. No hermeneutic, therefore, of which the historical Christ is not the focal point is acceptable. Holy Scripture must be treated as what it essentially is—the witness of the Father to the incarnate Son.

It appears that the Old Testament canon had been fixed by the time of Jesus. The New Testament canon is likewise now closed, inasmuch as no new apostolic witness to the historical Christ can now be borne. No new revelation (as distinct from Spirit-given understanding of existing revelation) will be given until Christ comes again. The canon was created in principle by divine inspiration. The Church's part was to discern the canon that God had created, not to devise one of its own.

The word *canon*, signifying a rule or standard, is a pointer to authority, which means the right to rule and control. Authority in Christianity belongs to God in His revelation, which means, on the one hand, Jesus Christ, the living Word, and, on the other hand, Holy Scripture, the written Word. But the authority of Christ and that of Scripture are one. As our Prophet, Christ testified that Scripture cannot be broken. As our Priest and King, He devoted His earthly life to fulfilling the law and the prophets, even dying in obedience to the words of messianic prophecy.

Thus as He saw Scripture attesting Him and His authority, so by His own submission to Scripture He attested its authority. As He bowed to His Father's instruction given in His Bible (our Old Testament), so He requires His disciples to do—not, however, in isolation but in conjunction with the apostolic witness to Himself that He undertook to inspire by His gift of the Holy Spirit. So Christians show themselves faithful servants of their Lord by bowing to the divine instruction given in the prophetic and apostolic writings that together make up our Bible.

By authenticating each other's authority, Christ and Scripture coalesce into a single fount of authority. The Biblically interpreted Christ and the Christ-centered, Christ-proclaiming Bible are from this standpoint one. As from the fact of inspiration we infer that what Scripture says, God says, so from the revealed relation between Jesus Christ and Scripture we may equally declare that what Scripture says, Christ says.

C. Infallibility, Inerrancy, Interpretation

Holy Scripture, as the inspired Word of God witnessing authoritatively to Jesus Christ, may properly be called *infallible* and *inerrant*. These negative terms have a special value, for they explicitly safeguard crucial positive truths.

Infallible signifies the quality of neither misleading nor being misled and so safeguards in categorical terms the truth that Holy Scripture is a sure, safe and reliable rule and guide in all matters.

Similarly, *inerrant* signifies the quality of being free from all falsehood or mistake and so safeguards the truth that Holy Scripture is entirely true and trustworthy in all its assertions.

We affirm that canonical Scripture should always be interpreted on the basis that it is infallible and inerrant. However, in determining what the God-taught writer is asserting in each passage, we must pay the most careful attention to its claims and character as a human production. In inspiration, God utilized the culture and conventions of his penman's milieu, a milieu that God controls in His sovereign providence; it is misinterpretation to imagine otherwise.

So history must be treated as history, poetry as poetry, hyperbole and metaphor as hyperbole and metaphor, generalization and approximation as what they are, and so forth. Differences between literary conventions in Bible times and in ours must also be observed: Since, for instance, nonchronological narration and imprecise citation were conventional and acceptable and violated no expectations in those days, we must not regard these things as faults when we find them in Bible writers. When total precision of a particular kind was not expected nor aimed at, it is no error not to have achieved it. Scripture is inerrant, not in the sense of being absolutely precise by modern standards, but in the sense of making good its claims and achieving that measure of focused truth at which its authors aimed.

The truthfulness of Scripture is not negated by the appearance in it of irregularities of grammar or spelling, phenomenal descriptions of nature, reports of false statements (e.g., the lies of Satan), or seeming discrepancies between one passage and another. It is not right to set the so-called "phenomena" of Scripture against the teaching of Scripture about itself. Apparent inconsistencies should not be ignored. Solution of them, where this can be convincingly achieved, will encourage our faith, and where for the present no convincing solution is at hand we shall significantly honor God by trusting His assurance that His Word is true, despite these appearances, and by maintaining our confidence that one day they will be seen to have been illusions.

Inasmuch as all Scripture is the product of a single divine mind, interpretation must stay within the bounds of the analogy of Scripture and eschew hypotheses that would correct one Biblical passage by another, whether in the name of progressive relation or of the imperfect enlightenment of the inspired writer's mind.

Although Holy Scripture is nowhere culture-bound in the sense that its teaching lacks universal validity, it is sometimes culturally conditioned by the customs and conventional views of a particular period, so that the application of its principles today calls for a different sort of action.

D. Skepticism and Criticism

Since the Renaissance, and more particularly since the Enlightenment, world views have been developed that involve skepticism about basic Christian tenets. Such are the agnosticism that denies that God is knowable, the rationalism that denies that He is incomprehensible, the idealism that denies that He is transcendent, and the existentialism that denies rationality in His relationships with us. When these un- and anti-Biblical principles seep into men's theologies at presuppositional level, as today they frequently do, faithful interpretation of Holy Scripture becomes impossible.

E. Transmission and Translation

Since God has nowhere promised an inerrant transmission of Scripture, it is necessary to affirm that only the autographic text of the original documents was inspired and to maintain the need of textual criticism as a means of detecting any slips that may have crept into the text in the course of its transmission. The verdict of this science, however, is that the Hebrew and Greek text appears to be amazingly well preserved, so that we are amply justified in affirming, with the Westminster Confession, a singular providence of God in this matter and in declaring that the authority of Scripture is in no way jeopardized by the fact that the copies we possess are not entirely error-free.

Similarly, no translation is or can be perfect, and all translations are an additional step away from the *autographa*. Yet the verdict of linguistic science is that English-speaking Christians, at least, are exceedingly well served in these days with a host of excellent translations and have no cause for hesitating to conclude that the true Word of God is within their reach. Indeed, in view of the frequent repetition in Scripture of the main matters with which it deals and also of the Holy Spirit's constant witness to and through the Word, no serious translation of Holy Scripture will so destroy its meaning as to render it unable to make its reader "wise for salvation through faith in Christ Jesus" (2 Tim 3:15).

F. Inerrancy and Authority

In our affirmation of the authority of Scripture as involving its total truth, we are consciously standing with Christ and His apostles, indeed with the whole Bible and with the main stream of Church history from the first days until very recently. We are concerned at the casual, inadvertent and seemingly thoughtless way in which a belief of such far-reaching importance has been given up by so many in our day.

We are conscious too that great and grave confusion results from ceasing to maintain the total truth of the Bible whose authority one professes to acknowledge. The result of taking this step is that the Bible that God gave loses its authority, and what has authority instead is a Bible reduced in content according to the demands of one's critical reasonings and in principle reducible still further once one has started. This means that at bottom independent reason now has authority, as opposed to Scriptural teaching. If this is not seen and if for the time being basic evangelical doctrines are still held, persons denying the full truth of Scripture may claim an evangelical identity while methodologically they have moved away from the evangelical principle of knowledge to an unstable subjectivism, and will find it hard not to move further.

Marsh

We affirm that what Scripture says, God says. May He
be glorified. Amen and Amen.

RECOMMENDED RESOURSES

I can envision someone overwhelmed at the prospect of not only reading the Bible but now encouraged to read *other books about reading the Bible*! The fact is, God has gifted the body of Christ with incredible teachers who have utilized their unique gifting in written works that help build the church (see Eph 4:11–12). To *study* Scripture does not merely mean to *read* it. Paul made it clear that Christians are to be "diligent" students of the Word (2 Tim 2:15).

This list of recommended resources for growing one's knowledge in Bible and hermeneutics is in no way exhaustive. I am quite aware that many worthwhile treatments are missing—the inevitable result whenever producing a list of anything valuable. What follows are resources that have personally benefited me and my teaching over the years, and ones that I feel are suitable for readers of this brief volume. The reader is encouraged not only to consult these works, but also the many more that are available and continue to be published each year.

Though only books are listed (many are available in electronic format), there are Bible software programs and websites that host scores of powerful tools to better understand the Bible. These include both paid subscriptions and free sites. The best subscription programs are Accordance Bible Software (Oak Tree Software, www.accordancebible.com), Logos Bible Software (Faithlife, www.logos.com), and Olive Tree Bible Software (www.olivetree.com). Several excellent free sites include: Bible.org (www.bible.org), Bible Hub (www.biblehub.com), Blue Letter Bible (www.blueletterbible.org), E-Sword (www.e-sword.net), Step Bible (www.stepbible.org), Bible Study Tools (www.biblestudytools.com), and Bible Gateway (www.biblegateway.com). Digital resources like these make accessibility to the Bible an undisputed reality in our twenty-first century world, eliminating any excuse for the "Christian to biblically illiterate."[1]

The resources below marked with a single * are print works I consider to be suitable for those newer to the field of bibliology (doctrine of the Bible) and hermeneutics. Those marked with a double ** are volumes I consider to be more suitable for intermediate to advanced levels. The reference works that follow these are those I consider perennially helpful for all levels of biblically literacy.

---

[1] Obviously, I have in mind the average American Christian as well as Christians living in countries where access to such technology is freely available. Until the Lord returns, there will remain the unfortunate reality of persecuted Christians living under oppressive regimes and governments who are not able to enjoy the same benefits.

Bibliology (Doctrine of the Bible)

Brake, Donald L. *A Visual History of the English Bible*. Grand Rapids: Baker 2008.*

Carson, D. A., ed. *The Enduring Authority of the Christian Scriptures*. Grand Rapids: Eerdmans, 2016.**

Carson, D. A., and John D. Woodbridge, eds. *Scripture and Truth*. Grand Rapids: Baker Academic, 1992.**

———. *Hermeneutics, Authority, and Canon*. Eugene: Wipf & Stock, 2005.**

Carson, D. A. *The King James Version Debate: A Plea for Realism*. Grand Rapids: Baker, 1978.**

Cowen, Steven B., and Terry L, eds. Wilder. *In Defense of the Bible: A Comprehensive Apologetic for the Authority of Scripture*. Nashville: B&H Academic, 2013.**

Dockery, David S. *Christian Scripture: An Evangelical Perspective on Inspiration, Authority, and Interpretation*. Eugene: Wipf & Stock, 1995.**

Frame, John. *The Doctrine of the Word of God*. A Theology of Lordship, vol 4. Phillipsburg, NJ: P&R, 2010.**

Geisler, Norman, ed. *Inerrancy*. Grand Rapids: Zondervan, 1980.**

Geisler, Norman L., and William E. Nix. *A General Introduction to the Bible*. Chicago: Moody, 1986. **

Geisler, Norman L., and William E. Nix. *From God to Us: How We Got Our Bible.* Rev. and exp. ed. Chicago: Moody, 2012.*

Gundry, Stanley, ed., *Five Views on Biblical Inerrancy.* Grand Rapids: Zondervan, 2013.**

Harris, Robert Laird. *Inspiration and Canonicity of the Bible: An Historical and Exegetical Study.* Grand Rapids: Zondervan, 1971. **

Hays, J. Daniel, and J. Scott Duvall, eds. *The Illustrated Bible Handbook.* Grand Rapids: Baker, 2020.*

House, H. Wayne and Timothy J. Demy. *Answers to Common Questions About the Bible.* Grand Rapids, MI: Kregel, 2014.*

Lindsell, Harold. *The Battle for the Bible.* Grand Rapids: Zondervan, 1980.*

MacArthur, John, ed. *The Inerrant Word: Biblical, Historical, Theological, and Pastoral Perspectives.* Wheaton: Crossway, 2016.*

Ward, Mark. *Authorized: The Use and Misuse of the King James Bible.* Bellingham: Lexham Press, 2018.*

Warfield. Benjamin Breckinridge. *The Inspiration and Authority of the Bible.* Phillipsburg, NJ: P&R, 2020.**

White, James. *The King James Only Controversy: Can You Trust Modern Translations?* Minneapolis: Bethany House, 2009.**

Woodbridge, John D. *Biblical Authority: Infallibility and Inerrancy in the Christian Tradition.* Grand Rapids: Zondervan Academic, 2015.**

Hermeneutics (History, Theory, and Practice of Interpreting Scripture)

Adler, Mortimer J., and Charles Van Doren. *How to Read a Book: The Classic Guide to Intelligent Reading.* New York: Simon and Schuster, 1972.* (Though this work only tangentially addresses reading Scripture, its concepts are of perennial help for general hermeneutics).

Blanchard, John. *How to Enjoy Your Bible: A Simple, Reliable, Clear, Substantial Resource.* Webster: Evangelical Press, 2007.*

Bauer, David R. and Robert A. Traina. *Inductive Bible Study: A Comprehensive Guide to the Practice of Hermeneutics.* Grand Rapids: Baker, 2014.*

Bock, Darrell L., and Buist M. Fanning. *Interpreting the New Testament Text: Introduction to the Art and Science of Exegesis.* Wheaton, IL: Crossway, 2006.**

Bray, Gerald. *Biblical Interpretation: Past & Present.* Downers Grove: Intervarsity, 1996.**

Carson, D. A. *Exegetical Fallacies*, 2nd ed. Grand Rapids: Baker, 1999.**

Casillas, Ken. *Beyond Chapter and Verse: The Theology and Practice of Biblical Application.* Eugene, OR: Wipf & Stock, 2018.*

Chou, Abner. *The Hermeneutics of the Biblical Writers: Learning to Interpret Scripture from the Prophets and Apostles.* Grand Rapids: Kregel, 2018.**

Cone, Christopher. *Priority in Biblical Hermeneutics and Theological Method.* Raymore: Exegetica, 2018.**

Couch, Mal, ed. *An Introduction to Classical Evangelical Hermeneutics: A Guide to the History and Practice of Biblical Interpretation.* Grand Rapids: Kregel, 2000.**

Duvall, J. Scott, and Daniel J. Hays. *Grasping God's Word: A Hands-on Approach to Reading, Interpreting, and Applying the Bible.* 4th ed. Grand Rapids: Zondervan, 2020.*

Fee, Gordon D. and Douglas Stuart. *How to Read the Bible for All Its Worth.* Grand Rapids: Zondervan, 2003.*

Fuhr, Richard Alan, and Andreas J. Köstenberger. *Inductive Bible Study: Observation, Interpretation, and Application through the Lenses of History, Literature, and Theology.* Nashville: B&H Academic, 2016.*

Grudem, Wayne, C. John Collins, and Thomas Schreiner, eds. *Understanding Scripture: An Overview of the Bible's Origin, Reliability, and Meaning.* Wheaton, IL: Crossway, 2012.*

Hendricks, Howard G. and William D. Hendricks. *Living by the Book: The Art and Science of Reading the Bible.* Chicago: Moody, 2007.*

Hirsch, E. D., *Validity in Interpretation.* New Haven: Yale University Press, 1967.** (Hirsch's volume is concerned with hermeneutics in general, but his principles are incredibly helpful and applicable for biblical hermeneutics).

House, Wayne H. and Forrest Weiland. *The Theory and Practice of Biblical Hermeneutics: Essays in Honor of Elliot Johnson.* Silverton, OR: Lampion, 2015.**

Johnson, Elliot E. *Expository Hermeneutics: An Introduction.* Grand Rapids: Zondervan, 1990. **

Kaiser, Walter C. and Moises Silva. *Introduction to Biblical Hermeneutics: The Search for Meaning.* Grand Rapids: Zondervan, 2007. **

Köstenberger, Andreas J. with Richard D. Patterson. *Invitation to Biblical Interpretation: Exploring the Hermeneutical Triad of History, Literature, and Theology.* 2nd ed. Grand Rapids: Kregel, 2020. **

———. *For the Love of God's Word: An Introduction to Biblical Interpretation.* Grand Rapids: Kregel, 2015.*

Neil, Stephen, and Tom Wright. *The Interpretation of the New Testament 1861–1986.* New York: Oxford University Press, 2003.**

Osborne, Grant R. *The Hermeneutical Spiral: A Comprehensive Introduction to Biblical Interpretation.* Downers Grove: InterVarsity Press, 2006. **

Plummer, Robert L. *40 Questions About Interpreting the Bible.* 2nd ed. Grand Rapids: Kregel Academic, 2021.*

Porter, Stanley E., and Jason C. Robinson. *Hermeneutics: An Introduction to Interpretive Theory.* Grand Rapids: Eerdmans, 2011.**

Porter, Stanley E., and Sean A. Adams. *Pillars in the History of Biblical Interpretation.* McMaster Biblical Studies 2. 2 vols. Eugene, OR: Pickwick, 2016.**

Poythress, Vern S. *God-centered Biblical Interpretation.* Phillipsburg, NJ: P&R Publishing, 1999.*

Ramm, Bernard. *Protestant Biblical Interpretation*, 3rd ed. Grand Rapids: Baker, 1970.*

Ryken, Leland. *How to Read the Bible as Literature.* Grand Rapids: Zondervan Academic, 1984.*

Silva, Moisés. *God, Language and Scripture: Reading the Bible in the Light of General Linguistics.* Grand Rapids: Zondervan, 1990.**

Sire, James W. *How to Read Slowly: Reading for Comprehension.* Colorado Springs: Waterbrook, 2009.* (Sire's volume is much like Adler/Van Doren's but more condensed and written from an evangelical perspective).

Sproul, R. C. *Knowing Scripture.* Downers Grove, IL: InterVarsity, 2016.*

Stein, Robert H. *A Basic Guide to Interpreting the Bible.* 2nd ed. Grand Rapids: Baker, 2011.*

Stuart, Douglas. *Old Testament Exegesis: A Handbook for Students and Pastors.* Louisville: Westminster, John Knox, 2009.**

Terry, Milton Spencer. *Biblical Hermeneutics: A Treatise on the Interpretation of the Old and New Testaments.* New York: Eaton & Mains, 1883; 2nd ed., Eugene: Wipf & Stock, 2003.**

Thomas, Robert L. *Evangelical Hermeneutics: The New Versus the Old.* Grand Rapids: Kregel, 2002.**

Virkler, Henry A., and Karelynne Gerber Ayayo. *Hermeneutics: Principles and Processes of Biblical Interpretation.* 2nd ed. Grand Rapids: Baker Academic, 2007.*

Wright, N. T. *Scripture and the Authority of God: How to Read the Bible Today.* San Francisco: HarperOne, 2013.*

Zuck, Roy B. *Basic Bible Interpretation: A Practical Guide to Discovering Biblical Truth.* Colorado Springs: David C. Cook, 1991.*

Reference Works for Bible (single-volume dictionaries, backgrounds, surveys, concordances)

Archer, Gleason L. *A Survey of Old Testament Introduction.* Chicago: Moody, 2007.

Arterbury, Andrew E., W. H. Bellinger Jr., and Derek S. Dodson. *Engaging the Christian Scriptures: An Introduction to the Bible.* 2nd ed. Grand Rapids: Baker Academic, 2021.

Beitzle, Barry, ed. *The New Moody Atlas of the Bible.* Chicago: Moody, 2009.

Carson, D. A., and Douglas J. Moo. *Introduction to the New Testament.* Grand Rapids: Zondervan Academic, 2007.

Freedman, David Noel, ed. *Eerdmans Dictionary of the Bible.* Grand Rapids: Eerdmans, 2000.

Harbin, Michael H. *The Promise and the Blessing: A Historical Survey of the Old and New Testaments.* Grand Rapids: Zondervan Academic, 2005.

House, Paul R., and Eric Mitchell. *Old Testament Survey.* 2nd ed. Nashville: B&H Academic, 2007.

Jensen, Irving L. *Jensen's Survey of the New Testament.* Chicago: Moody, 1981.

———. *Jensen's Survey of the Old Testament.* Chicago: Moody, 1978.

Keener, Craig. *The IVP Bible Background Commentary: New Testament.* 2nd ed. Downers Grove: IVP Academic, 2014.

Kohlenberger, John R. III, Edward W. Goodrick, and James A. Swanson. *Greek-English Concordance to the New Testament.* Grand Rapids: Zondervan, 1997.

Kohlenberger, John R. III, and Swanson, James A. *The Hebrew-English Concordance to the Old Testament.* Grand Rapids: Zondervan, 1998.

Köstenberger, Andreas J., and Raymond Bouchoc. *The Book Study Concordance.* Grand Rapids: B&H Academic, 2003.

Köstenberger, Andreas J., L. Scott Kellum, and Charles L. Quarles. *The Cradle, The Cross, and the Crown: An Introduction to the New Testament.* 2nd ed. Nashville: B&H Academic, 2016.

Locker Sr., Herbert with F. F. Bruce and R. K. Harrison. *The Illustrated Bible Dictionary.* Nashville: Thomas Nelson, 1986.

Longman, Tremper III., and Raymond B. Dillard. *An Introduction to the Old Testament.* 2nd ed. Grand Rapids: Zondervan Academic, 2006.

Marshall, I. Howard, A. R Millard, J. I. Packer, D. J. Wiseman, eds. *The New Bible Dictionary.* 3rd ed. Downers Grove: Intervarsity, 1996.

Merrill, Eugene H., Mark Rooker, and Michael A. Grisanti: *The World and the Word: An Introduction to the Old Testament*. Nashville: B&H Academic, 2011.

Powell, Mark Allen. *Introducing the New Testament: A Historical, Literary, and Theological Survey*. 2nd ed. Grand Rapids: Baker Academic, 2018.

Stedman, Ray. *Adventuring through the Bible: Old Testament*. Grand Rapids: Our Daily Bread, 2016.

Strong, James, and W. E. Vine. *Strong's Concise Concordance and Vine's Concise Dictionary of The Bible*. Nashville: Thomas Nelson, 1999.

Thomas, Robert L. *The Strongest NASB Exhaustive Concordance*. Grand Rapids: Zondervan, 2004.

SCRIPTURE INDEX

Marsh

Made in the USA
Middletown, DE
13 May 2022